Twayne's United States Authors Series

Sylvia E. Bowman, *Editor*

INDIANA UNIVERSITY

James Boyd

JAMES BOYD

By DAVID E. WHISNANT
University of Illinois

 199

Twayne Publishers, Inc.   ::   New York

Preface

In 1931 Stanley Kunitz, who interviewed James Boyd, wrote that "Looking at him now—lean, brown and muscular . . . it is difficult to realize that doctors' orders to go South and live on his grandfather's plantation really transformed James Boyd, just discharged from the army, into an author." Kunitz quoted Boyd as saying, " 'I had to do something when I got down South . . . so I decided to try writing short stories.' "[1] Four years later Julian R. Meade reported in the *Saturday Review of Literature* that Boyd wrote short stories and novels "because he prefers it to other work and his Presbyterian training gave him the idea that 'every man has got to do something.' "[2] The legend of a war invalid who returned to the home of his ancestors and began to write partly to ease his Presbyterian conscience and partly to provide himself with an innocent diversion has achieved such wide currency in subsequent biographical and critical statements that it has heretofore been almost impossible to form an accurate estimation of either Boyd's career or his writings.[3]

The fact is that Boyd was serious about his writing; but, in his characteristically diffident way he rarely took himself very seriously in public; therefore, he neglected to create and to protect the kind of public image that most writers instinctively make. His novels were both critical and popular successes; but, when he was interviewed by newspaper or magazine reporters, he minimized the seriously artistic side of his personality and accentuated the "country squire" side reflected in most published statements about him.

If we look carefully at Boyd's works and at the documentary records of his career, however, we form a very different picture of him as a writer. The record shows clearly that, when he committed himself in 1920 to a five-year, self-imposed literary apprenticeship, he was continuing a serious interest in writing that he had had during his adolescence and his college years and beyond. Even after fifteen years of successful writing, during which he published four excellent novels and nearly two dozen short stories in such magazines as *Scribner's Monthly, American Mercury,* and *Harper's,* Boyd still felt that writing was like trying "to put a watch together in a dark room with only a ten-pound hammer [and] a tire iron" as tools.[4] The radiant visions in the writer's mind, he said, are seen "with such harmonious intricacy, such wealth and precision of detail that all attempts to transfer them into language can only be deemed . . . comparative failures."[5]

Late in his career, Boyd told Sherwood Anderson that "[if] I write no better it is because I can't. . . . My steadily declining sales may mean that I'm getting somewhere. Again it may not. In either case I don't assume that I could have kept my popularity if I'd wanted to, or that I deserve credit for having lost it. Like everybody else, I had to write the best I could."[6] A month later, Boyd described himself again to Anderson as a "baffled wanderer, trying to find the road that leads to better work, trying ludicrously maybe, to find for himself something that if found at all can only be found for him by the unknown god."[7] Similar opinions have frequently been voiced, of course, by other writers; they are recorded here not because they are assumed to be original but because they reveal Boyd's consistently serious attitude toward his work.

But the real question is, of course, neither Boyd's attitude toward his own work, nor his attitude toward his audience, nor theirs toward him; our problem is the actual quality of the things he wrote. How good are they? How well do the individual works stand up to analysis, and how substantial does his total work seem fifty years after his career began? What contributions did he make toward the refinement of the forms in which he worked? What are the facts of his literary career, and what importance attaches to them?

Since these questions have never been adequately discussed, the primary object of this study of Boyd is to discuss them in some detail. I have quoted extensively from Boyd's novels in order not only to make my assertions concrete and precise, but also to indicate the actual quality of prose in the novels. I have treated Boyd's poetry only slightly, for neither its quantity nor its quality justifies extensive commentary.

Chapter 1, a brief but comprehensive biographical statement, embraces the primary facts of Boyd's life both before and after he became a writer; it also traces the development of his mind insofar as it relates to his literary career. Chapter 2, an analysis of Boyd's early career as a short-story writer, concentrates on the years between 1920 and 1925 but includes some stories written as late as 1943. The emphasis is upon the stories themselves; for, although Boyd's literary reputation does not rest upon his stories, it is important to consider them because they indicate the direction of his developing interests and because they contain, in a few instances, some of his best writing.

Chapters 3, 4, and 5 are about the five novels: *Drums* (1925), *Marching On* (1927), *Long Hunt* (1930), *Roll River* (1935), and *Bitter Creek* (1939). I have departed from strict chronology in one instance, where I discuss *Long Hunt* and *Bitter Creek* as thematically related novels of the frontier in Chapter 4. The plan of treatment is virtually the same for every novel: brief attention is paid to the genesis of the novel, to the circumstances of its composition, to its sales and critical reception. A short plot summary is followed by extensive analysis of the novel, concluding with a section considering the work's specific merits as a historical novel. The overall aim of these final sections is to provide a cumulative assessment of Boyd's contribution to the development of the genre.

Chapter 6 is an analysis of the Free Company of Players, a radio drama group Boyd organized and directed just before World War II. The Free Company venture was important not only in Boyd's own career but also in the history of American literature; the account of it in Chapter 6, based on original documents, is the first to appear in print. Chapter 7 is a brief concluding statement about the general quality of Boyd's work and the significance of his career.

Although general histories of the American novel usually fail to mention Boyd's work,[8] it has long been recognized that his novels are generally superior to others of their type. In 1939 Bernard DeVoto asserted that they "are among the best of our time in America and they are by so far the best historical novels that no others seriously challenge their preëminence."[9] Recently, there have been indications that a substantial evaluation of Boyd's work is warranted,[10] but such an evaluation has for several reasons been delayed. Critical studies of the historical novel have unfortunately more often taken the form of lists of novels arranged by century than of intensive analysis of the best novels.[11]

More important, however, is the fact that the historical novel itself has usually been assumed to be an inferior form and therefore to be undeserving of discussion in general histories of the American novel. Bernard DeVoto made the point thirty years ago in a review of Boyd's *Roll River* (1935): "The fact that Mr. Boyd has hitherto concerned himself with the American past has sometimes obscured his great merits as a realist behind the popular conception of historical fiction as romantic. . . . [But] now there can be no easy dismissal of him as a period novelist."[12] Reviewers consistently recognized with DeVoto that, simply because Boyd's works could usually be described more or less accurately as "historical novels," they were not necessarily unsophisticated as works of art. But the persistent simplistic "conception of historical fiction as romantic" has become over the years a barrier against proper evaluation of Boyd's artistic accomplishment.

My general aim is, therefore, to evaluate Boyd's writings first of all as works of art in their own right, predicated on the same precise awareness of man's nature at one instant in time that one finds in Ernest Hemingway, F. Scott Fitzgerald, or Sherwood Anderson. Having done so, I propose to examine them as historically informed artistic statements. My thesis is that these two aspects of Boyd's work are complementary, not antagonistic, as has frequently been assumed.

In addition to Boyd's published writings, I have used heretofore unused major collections of correspondence, manuscripts, and typescripts in the Southern Historical Collection of the University of North Carolina, the Princeton University Library, and the files of Charles Scribner's Sons, Inc., Boyd's publisher. In addition, I have had access to materials still in the possession of Boyd's family. Paul Green, Boyd's closest friend for twenty-five years, also allowed me to consult his own diaries and personal correspondence.

I should like to thank the following libraries and individuals for their invaluable assistance in making these materials available to me: Duke University Library; Dr. Jerrold Orne and Miss Anna Brooke Allan of the University of North Carolina Library; Dr. Alexander P. Clark of the Princeton University

Preface

Library; the University of Illinois Library; the public library of Southern Pines, North Carolina; and Charles Scribner, Jr., of Charles Scribner's Sons, Inc. I am also indebted to the following libraries and institutions for supplying invaluable technical assistance and copies of Boyd materials in their collections: the Berg Collection of the New York Public Library; Houghton Library of Harvard University; the University of Virginia Library; Saint John's Seminary of Camarillo, California; the Pennsylvania State Library; the University of Michigan Library; Pack Memorial Public Library of Asheville, North Carolina; the Hill School Library; and the Historical Society of Dauphin County, Pennsylvania.

Many individuals who knew or who were related to James Boyd have provided information and assistance I could have obtained nowhere else. Boyd's widow Katharine Lamont Boyd has provided unfailing interest and support since the inception of the project, as has his brother Jackson Herr Boyd. Among Boyd's former friends and associates who volunteered useful information are George Jones, Marion Sims Wyeth, Charles W. Norman, and Frederick Osborn.

For financial support during various stages of my work I am grateful to the Woodrow Wilson Foundation, the Danforth Foundation, and the Graduate School of Arts and Sciences of Duke University and of the University of Illinois. Finally, I should like to thank Professor Richard Walser, who graciously assisted me in beginning my work on James Boyd; my colleague James Hurt, who read the entire manuscript and made many useful suggestions for improvement; and Professor Arlin Turner, whose patience and wise counsel have been of incalculable benefit since the first stages of my work. Cora Scholz prepared an immaculate typescript from a nearly illegible manuscript.

D. E. W.

Urbana, Illinois
September, 1967

Acknowledgments

Permission to quote for publication has been generously granted by the following individuals, libraries, publishers, and periodicals:

The University of North Carolina Library. James Boyd manuscripts and correspondence in the Southern Historical Collection.

The Princeton University Library. Manuscripts in the Boyd Collection.

Charles Scribner's Sons, Inc. Quotations from Boyd's published works; from Elizabeth Nowell (ed.), *The Letters of Thomas Wolfe* (1956); from John Hall Wheelock (ed.), *Editor to Author: the Letters of Maxwell Perkins* (1950); and from one manuscript letter from James Boyd to Maxwell Perkins.

The University of North Carolina Press. Quotations from Robert A. Lively, *Fiction Fights the Civil War* (1957); and from James Boyd, *Old Pines and Other Stories* (1952).

Dodd, Mead & Company. Quotations from James Boyd (ed.), *The Free Company Presents* (1941).

Saturday Review. Quotations from articles and reviews by Bernard DeVoto and Julian R. Meade.

Little, Brown & Company. Quotations from one letter in Howard M. Jones and Walter B. Rideout (eds.), *Letters of Sherwood Anderson.* Copyright 1953, by Eleanor Anderson.

The *Atlantic.* Quotations from one Boyd poem, "Echoes of Earth."

Paul Green. Quotation from one letter, July 19, 1943.

Katharine L. Boyd. Quotations from James Boyd's published works, manuscripts, and correspondence.

Contents

Chronology

1888   James Boyd born July 2, in Harrisburg, Pennsylvania, the son of Eleanor Herr and John Yeomans Boyd.

1901   Enters the Hill School, Pottstown, Pennsylvania; begins to spend brief periods in North Carolina.

1904   First short story published in the Hill School *Record*. Other stories and poems published 1904-6. Boyds establish a permanent residence in North Carolina.

1906   Receives Alfred Raymond Memorial Prize for short story. Graduates from the Hill School, June. Enters Princeton University, September.

1910   Graduates from Princeton University. Works as staff writer and cartoonist for Harrisburg *Patriot*, June-August. Enters Trinity College, Cambridge, October.

1912   Receives degree from Trinity College. Joins faculty of Harrisburg Academy, September. Teaches until following summer. Forced by illness to decline second year of teaching.

1913   Spends entire year in Southern Pines, North Carolina. Except for brief periods, lives in North Carolina until fall of 1916.

1914   Confined by illness to Watkins Glen Sanatarium (New York), July-September. Returns to Southern Pines.

1915   Attends National Guard Camp at Tobyhanna, Pennsylvania, August. Begins series of attempts, despite illness, to go on active military duty.

1916   Enlists in New York Artillery, July 5; discharged for medical reasons. Joins editorial staff of *Country Life in America*, September 6. Works until late January.

1917   Works as volunteer with American Red Cross, helping to procure ambulances for war service. Commissioned second lieutenant in United States Army Ambulance Service, August 28. Marries Katharine Lamont, December 15.

1918   Arrives in Italy in July as commander of Ambulance Service Section 520. Transferred to France August 28. Participates in Saint Mihiel campaign, and first and second Meuse-Argonne offensives September through November. Assists in rationing civilian population, Montmédy, France, November 11-December 22.

1919   Hospitalized in France several times before being sent home in March; discharged July 2. Decides to become a writer.

1920   Moves to Southern Pines. First story ("The Sound of a Voice") accepted by *Scribner's Magazine*, September 29.

1921   First story ("Old Pines") published in *Century Magazine,*
       March. Eleven stories published by 1925.

1922   Begins first novel.

1925   *Drums* published March 27. Begins Civil War novel.

1927   *Marching On* published in spring. Begins novel of the frontier.

1930   *Long Hunt* published. Begins fourth novel. Completion de-
       layed by illness and series of operations, 1930-34.

1935   *Roll River* published April 25.

1937   Elected to National Institute of Arts and Letters.

1939   *Bitter Creek* published, March. Elected charter member of
       Society of American Historians, February.

1941   Establishes Free Company of Players. Series of radio dramas
       broadcast nationwide, February 23-May 4. Plays published
       as *The Free Company Presents* (1941). Buys and becomes
       editor of Southern Pines *Pilot.*

1943   First poem, "Song for the Silent," published in the *Atlantic
       Monthly,* May.

1944   Dies in Princeton, New Jersey, February 25. *Eighteen Poems*
       (1944) published posthumously.

CHAPTER 1

A Biographical Introduction

JAMES Boyd's name is generally associated with North Carolina, but for two centuries his family were Pennsylvanians. Not until after 1900 did the Boyds establish a residence in North Carolina, and James Boyd himself lived there little until after he was grown. The first generation of Boyds, emigrating from Ireland, settled in Chester County in the early eighteenth century; succeeding generations migrated west through the Lebanon and Susquehanna River valleys. John Cowen Boyd was born in Danville, on the east fork of the Susquehanna, near the end of the eighteenth century. His son James, grandfather of the novelist, was born there in 1831.[1]

In 1849, James Boyd joined the survey corps of the Shamokin and Pottsville Railroad, about twenty miles southwest of Danville. He soon began floating barges of coal by canal from nearby Sunbury to the Chesapeake Bay. It was a risky venture, but it was also a propitious time to get into the coal business. Several newly opened mines at Shamokin soon passed into Boyd's control, and became the nucleus of a mining and distribution operation that eventually supplied much of the coal used by the Pennsylvania Railroad.

In 1861, Boyd married Louisa Yeomans, daughter of the Reverend John Williams Yeomans, moderator of the general assembly of the Presbyterian Church. The coal business, spurred by the Civil War and by the ensuing industrial boom, continued to prosper. In 1873, James Boyd moved his offices and his family, which now included a twelve-year-old son, John Yeomans Boyd, to the state capital, Harrisburg. John Boyd went east to the College of New Jersey in 1880, returning four years later to join his father's business. In 1887 he married Eleanor Gilmore Herr, daughter of Andrew Jackson Herr, lawyer and member of the state Senate. Their first son James, born July 2, 1888, was named for his paternal grandfather.

John Boyd was a man of business and of the church; and
the Harrisburg of the last decade of the nineteenth century, in
which James Boyd grew up, granted its unqualified approbation
to the combination of financial success, social respectability,
and Christian piety that he embodied. In him the gospel of
wealth found full expression. Grandson of a clergyman thrice
awarded honorary doctorates for service to the Presbyterian
Church, John Boyd became an elder in Harrisburg's fashionable Pine Street Presbyterian Church, and was for years super-
intendent of its Sunday school, which he built into the largest
in the city. At his death, his will provided for adding the John
Y. Boyd recreational and educational wing to the Pine Street
Church. His highest ecclesiastical honor was perhaps his elec-
tion to the board of trustees of the Princeton Theological
Seminary.

Boyd's success as a businessman more than matched his
eminence as a churchman. Within a few years after he had
entered the family business, he had become president of Tyrone
Iron Company; a director of the Elk River Coal and Lumber
Company and of Harrisburg's First National Bank; and, of
course, a principal officer in James Boyd & Company. He was
on the governing boards of numerous charitable institutions,
and in 1908 he was appointed by Governor Stuart to a term
on the Pennsylvania Railroad Commission. At his death in
1914, the Harrisburg *Telegraph* estimated his estate to be
"several millions."

John Boyd's life involved the central ironies of the society
in which James Boyd grew up—ironies that were not only
tolerated but actually celebrated. The Harrisburg Centennial
celebration of 1885 was a public tribute to the piety, respectability, and patriotism that were assumed to be natural by-
products of the expansion of industry under free enterprise. On
Industrial Display Day, all the "fresh-looking, sturdy thorough-
bred American" children were dismissed from school; and in
the "grandest parade ever witnessed ... the boy whose father
can count his money by the thousands marched linked arms
with the lad whose father works for ninety cents a day as a
laborer. And they both wore the American flag on their bosoms."[2]
The chief attractions of the parade were the floats of local
manufacturers and merchants. One was a butcher shop on wheels,
pulled by four horses: "The wagon was handsomely draped,

and on it [was] a sausage machine in full operation, with butcher George M. Hiller handing out excellent bologna sausage along the route.... The wagon was labelled, 'The old and the new way.' "[3]

The whole spectacle exuded confidence that all old ways were indeed gone forever and that the new way promised prosperity to all who deserved it. Harrisburg citizens had merely to await a glorious materialistic future whose arrival would incidentally assure their souls' salvation. Of the fact that cotton-mill hands were being paid seven cents an hour for a sixty-hour week, the less said the better.[4] James Boyd was heir to a tradition that he would find himself less and less able to accept, but he never forgot its ironies. His novel *Roll River*, published fifty years after the centennial, is built largely on the "beautiful and simple and symbolic" ironies of life in Harrisburg.[5]

The Boyds lived elegantly in the most respectable of Harrisburg's neighborhoods. For them, good taste seems to have borne a tacit relationship to a state of grace. They maintained three town houses in the fashionable section between the Capitol and the Susquehanna River—Grandfather Boyd's brownstone on Front Street, Aunt Helen Dull's at the corner of Pine and Front, and John Boyd's at 124 Pine Street. From Thanksgiving until May, they lived in town; the summers were spent in "Oakleigh," a massive, gray stone country house north of town.

I *Hill School*

James Boyd's frailty as a child made it necessary for him to be tutored at home for the first years of his schooling; but when he was twelve, his father decided to send him away to preparatory school. Later, John Boyd assumed, his son would go to Princeton, and then would return to join the family business and to establish himself in Harrisburg society. Boyd himself was a trustee of the Harrisburg Academy, but he chose to send James to the Hill School, whose headmaster John Meigs, "servant of Christ, master of boys, maker of men," was committed to the principles of "obedience, honor, physical training as an aid to moral soundness and intellectual growth, public service as an obligation of privilege, and religious faith and loyalty."[6]

Although James Boyd later described Hill as "a chocolate brown institution, inculcating muscular Christianity,"[7] he at first embraced the Meigsian ethic. He held office in the Young Men's Christian Association; attended daily chapel; and, by his own admission, found "a good deal of pleasure and help in looking up [in the Bible] what the ministers have preached about."[8] Boyd ranked first in his class the first year, second the next year, but ninth the following year. To a reprimand from his father, he responded, "[I am] dissatisfied with myself as I have never been before. I'm glad you wrote me that way because it's time I was waking up and getting in the game."[9]

The metaphor of life as a game to be played according to rules dictated by the Almighty was frightening, considering the consequences of losing, but Boyd soon discovered that it could also be played according to a different set of rules. "The good news has come at last," he wrote to his mother a few months later, "I am going to Africa as a missionary where I shall introduce the game of hockey to the natives."[10] The "muscular Christianity" that John Boyd thought would groom his son for the game of life was already revealing its essential inadequacy; James Boyd had not yet spoken his *non serviam*, but his natural buoyancy and intellectual curiosity were beginning to lead him away from the bland piety outlined by Meigs.

During Boyd's last two years at Hill, he began to write short stories, poems, and plays. With his classmate Merrell Clement he wrote and played a leading role in *To Him Who Waits*, a three-act comedy produced by the dramatic club. His best short story, "Little Sister," which received the Alfred Raymond Memorial Prize, was full of juvenile sentimentality ("Gentle she was withal; yet never fearing..."), but it also contained occasional graphic phrases: "a long slit of sunlight flittering in between the shutters and falling slantwise on the counterpane."[11]

In his final year, Boyd was class poet and editor-in-chief of the literary magazine. In the class poem, a rather melancholy Neoclassical first stanza ("Upon Neritus stood young Odysseus...") is followed by an abrupt shift in tone and cadence: "Arm, arm, arm,/ Thou soldier of the world...." From the commencement platform Boyd intoned the final stanza:

> Die, die, die,
>   When thou has spent thy might.
> Death cannot hold the spirit bold
>   That falls amid the fight;

> On other fields he fights nor yields,
> Who dies here for the right.[12]

The melodrama is not surprising from an eighteen-year-old, and the moral tone that overlays the military metaphor is singularly appropriate for Boyd's upbringing.

II *Princeton and Cambridge*

In September, 1906, Boyd entered Princeton University, which, under its new President Woodrow Wilson, was becoming far less provincial than it had been when his father had graduated. Boyd's courses the first two years were primarily the Latin, Greek, French, and mathematics required of all bachelor-of-arts students. As a freshman, he joined only the Hill School Club and the Pennsylvania Club, and apparently took part in few other activities. In deference to his father's wishes, he took a variety of practical courses—physics, chemistry, political science, architectural drawing, geodesy, and money and banking—but his interests became increasingly literary from his junior year onward.

In a letter Boyd wrote to his mother during the winter of 1908, he refers to a letter by Thomas Macaulay, written at age fourteen, "which might serve as an example for James age 19."[13] Macaulay's letter to Mrs. Hannah More, a collection of precocious comments on literature, concludes, "I pride myself upon being able to say that there are many readers of the *Christian Observer* who could do without Walter Scott's works, but not without those of, my dear Madam, your affectionate friend, Thomas B. Macaulay."[14] Equally revealing is Mrs. More's subsequent letter to Macaulay's father about his son's intellectual and literary development. "The quantity of reading that Tom has poured in," she said, "and the quantity of writing he has poured out, is astonishing. . . . We have poetry for breakfast, dinner, and supper. . . . His fine promise of mind expands more and more, and, what is extraordinary, he has as much accuracy in his expression as spirit and vivacity in his imagination. . . . I encourage him to live much in the open air; this . . . I hope, will invigorate his body; though his frail body is sometimes tired, the spirits are never exhausted."[15]

Boyd himself was writing poetry, although apparently none was published, and few of his friends knew about his efforts. He did, however, show some of his poems to a young English

instructor, Struthers Burt. "I had heard that there was an
especially brilliant junior, a man who wrote far above the
average," Burt said, "and then one day Jim Boyd came to see
me.... [We] sat out on the veranda and talked all afternoon.
... Finally, he told me shyly that he had written some poetry
and would like to show it to me."[16]

One of the poems Boyd read to Burt may have been the
short melancholy lyric left in manuscript in the Boyd collection
at Princeton:

> No one to see the sun on distant hills
> Or watch with me the quiet browns of fall
> No one to share the breathless twilight hour
> When evening's truce of God steals over all—
>
> Only the shadow of a dream remains,
> Dream shadows of a magic moment, flown.
> All else is vanished. Toward the waiting years
> Forward, I march, alone.[17]

Compared with the "Death cannot hold the spirit bold" class
poem, this poem is still self-conscious; but the technique is
surer: it still employs the melodramatic military metaphor, but
the moral tone has been supplanted by a melancholia which,
if no less mannered, is at least organic to the subject.

Throughout his years at Princeton, Boyd remained submissive
and even, to a degree, sympathetic to the conservatism of his
parents. After a meeting of the editorial board of the humor
magazine near the end of his junior year, he wrote to his mother
that "The motion to drop liquor advertisements was lost in
spite of all I could do."[18] He was also still preparing himself
somewhat vaguely for a business career. He kept on with his
poetry, however, despite his parents' plans for his career.
By the end of his senior year, he had gained considerable poetic
skill, as his sonnet "Commencement—1910" shows:

> Under the street lamps, antic figures weave
> In motley, and the mild June night is rent
> With pulsing bands and noisy make believe
> Of fellowship within a shadowy tent:
> Hoarse songs and calls and stamping on the floor
> The crash of glass, the tramp of marching feet,
> Laughter and shouts, a dull unmeaning roar
> Rolling now loud now faintly down the street.

The air grows still, as sea stills after storms
Silent the town, the cool moon-shadows fall
Across the dim-lit campus and the forms
Of tigers keeping watch at Nassau Hall;
Silent, save where two friends long parted greet—
And there the strength and peace of Princeton meet.[19]

Near the end of his final year at Princeton, Boyd decided to go on to Trinity College, Cambridge, for a master's degree in English literature, but his actual departure was delayed for three months because his parents were reluctant to give their permission. To pass the time and no doubt to avoid becoming involved in the coal business, he took a job for the summer with the Harrisburg *Patriot*. Since many of the regular staff were on vacation, Boyd was man-of-all-work: cartoonist, military reporter, human-interest writer, and sports reporter. His first article appeared on July 14. Subsequent articles, illustrated with his own pen drawings and cartoons, appeared regularly until early in September.

Toward the end of the summer, John Boyd, who neither liked nor understood his son's preference for the arts, finally gave his permission for a year of literary study at Trinity College. Boyd landed in Paris in late September and met his Princeton friend George Jones, who accompanied him to England.[20] At Trinity, the two took rooms at 9 Jesus Lane, overlooking the gardens of Sidney Sussex College. Betraying the genteel snobbery of his upbringing, Boyd told his parents that the furnishings were "typical English middle-class & not quite the kind we would select for ourselves."[21] He became involved in the life of the college immediately, however. Such spartan rituals as the cold morning bath, which, as an institution, he said, "rivals the Bank of England," functioned as a secular baptism to make him "at last . . . a true Englishman."[22]

Boyd signed up initially for a series of courses that split his time between trying to please his father and trying to pursue his own interests: a law course ("Estates in Land") and a course in Restoration literature, an economics course ("Company Finance and Stock Exchange") and a course in Romantic literature. Within a few days, however, he substituted Professor Skeat's course in Anglo-Saxon and Middle English for the law course, and he told his father he was merely "clinging to Company Finance as the last shred of respectability."[23]

Making a place for himself socially at Trinity was more difficult than his experience at Princeton had led him to expect.
Although most of the desirable social clubs were not open to
American students, Boyd joined rowing and debating groups,
and he made friends in the Officer's Training Corps. The latter
interested him intensely. "It is hard to believe that there is any
place in England that looks so like Montana as Salisbury Plain,"
he wrote after his unit's maneuvers at the end of the year. "There
is no farming there; only the great brown plain broken by low
ridges and here and there a dark green cluster of trees." It was
splendid, he said, "to see the horse artillery coming into action
...the gunners black with oil and powder, [working] like
demons slamming shell after shell into the smoking breeches."[24]

Boyd had originally told his parents he had "not the slightest
intention"[25] of remaining for a second year at Cambridge, but
during the winter of 1911 he decided to do so.[26] The following
October his friend Fred Osborn arrived, and the two moved
to rooms in New Court. Their main diversion during the year
was fox-hunting. Boyd had never hunted before he came to
England, but after his first ride to hounds he hunted regularly
for the rest of his life.[27] Dressed in heavy black tailcoat, derby
hat, black boots, and brown britches, he and Osborn usually
hunted with the Fitzwilliam and Cambridgeshire hunts.

The effect of the first hunt on Boyd's imagination is evident
in an account he wrote twenty years later as an introduction to
Anthony Trollope's *Hunting Sketches*. The hunt took place at
Christmas, near the village of Cattistock:

The mist [hung] over the thatched roofs of the single winding street,
over the wet slates of the minor gentry and the tawny, blunted spire
of the withdrawn church, over the Master's house in its modest park
and the kennels on the Southern hillside. . . . Up ahead, a cluster
of scarlet showed where the pillars of the hunt foregathered nearest
to the Master and the hounds.
    He was the Reverend Mr. Milne, the sporting parson. . . .
    "Now then, hounds, gentlemen, please!" We were off to draw
the gorse. Below us stretched the hedgerows, the cottage chimneys
and the wet, still beech woods. . . .
    That evening at tea-time a note came to the house. . . . [I] was
asked to dine with the Master. . . .
    Over the port he eyed me.

"How old are you?"

"Twenty-one."

"How long have you been hunting?"

"This was my first day."

His kind, shrewd face fell into brooding lines. His eyes took on the sombre light of the true faith. With his pipe-stem he tapped me on the knee:

"Fifteen years of your life have been thrown away."[28]

Since midway in Boyd's first year at Cambridge, he had felt the urgency of deciding what he was to do when he finished his course. "I am entering upon the best years of [my] life," he told his parents, "and [I] must not delay much longer." He knew he was expected eventually to come home to help manage the estate, but he was not interested. He applied for a preceptorship at Princeton; and when no openings were available, he considered taking a job with a publishing house.[29] An opportunity to teach at the Harrisburg Academy seemed attractive, and he asked his father to investigate it. John Boyd not only investigated but apparently nearly took over the academy in order to promote his son's interest. Boyd was so distressed that he refused to consider the opportunity until he persuaded his father to withdraw.[30] Satisfied that he had done so, he applied for the job. Near the middle of April, 1912, he submitted his university thesis, wrote to accept the job, and arranged for passage home.[31]

Reflecting on his two years at Cambridge as he sailed home, Boyd filled forty pages of ship's stationery. What did it all mean? How valuable had it been? He had found that the pattern of life at Cambridge had provided but small physical comfort, and the system of instruction to be "wasteful and cumbersome," but understandably so, since "the universities are designed for men with money, [and] there is no particular reason for practicing economy." The Englishman tolerates "the high cost and relatively small comfort of his life in the University," Boyd observed, "because he is not really paying for physical comfort at all—he is paying for independence. It would be cheaper for him to share his room with another man, but he is not willing even to save money at the price of his own liberty. . . . [The] whole of the Englishman's college life is arranged so as to give him the greatest possible freedom in controlling his [own] movements. . . ."[32]

Boyd had found that freedom a welcome replacement for the rigidities of his early life in Harrisburg, for the bland pieties of Hill School, and for the oppressive social stuffiness of Princeton social clubs, modeled as they were on the fashionable society into which members presumably passed after graduation. The question for Boyd was whether he would finally enter that system or go another way. He suspected that managing the Boyd estate was not his appointed place in life, but he was unsure what that place was.

III *Interval of Unrest*

The Harrisburg Academy was small—twelve teachers and barely a hundred students—but Boyd found his job challenging. He taught English and French and coached the athletic teams; but his health, which had never been very good, deteriorated markedly by the end of the year. Fatigued and depressed, he did not return to the academy. In March, 1914, his father died, and the responsibility for the estate descended upon him and his brother Jackson. But Boyd contracted a mild case of infantile paralysis in midsummer, and while he underwent treatment at Watkins Glen, New York, during the late summer and early fall, Jackson was appointed sole executor.

During the interval after Boyd's teaching in Harrisburg, and for more than two years after his illness, he lived quietly on a large farm his grandfather had bought near the turn of the century in Moore County, North Carolina. He had first stayed there during the winter of 1904 when illness had forced him to withdraw from Hill School for several months. Boyd's attraction to the area increased during subsequent visits. In 1913 he said, "This is really the most beautiful country I know.... [It] has a certain wildness without being desolate. You get the effect of solitude without loneliness.... There is ... thank heaven no cheap pseudosmart Harrisburg Society."[33]

As he regained his strength, Boyd read a great deal, helped to manage the farm and the affairs of his father's estate, and resumed his fox-hunting. "The last few months have seen me swamped with estate business and a pack of hounds," he wrote to his Cambridge friend Charles Norman. "The latter are eating up the substance of the former & I am forced to realize that I am equally ignorant about both."[34] As Boyd began to realize that the life he was living in the South seemed to lead "nowhere in particular," he began also to feel again the urgency of setting upon a career. He had considered the publishing field while he was at Cambridge, and later he and Jackson had investigated taking jobs with the Princeton University Press—"[Jackson] on the business end & I on the literary," as he told his parents[35]—so when his new friend from Moore County, Frank Page, offered him an editorial position with the Doubleday, Page Company, he accepted. In September, 1916, he moved to New York to join the staff of *Country Life in America*, then published by Doubleday, Page. In December, he wrote to Charles Norman that "in the course of a year" he would decide whether to continue or to return to North Carolina. Going back to Harrisburg was by this time out of the question.[36]

Boyd liked his work at Doubleday, but his attention was turning more and more toward the war in Europe. Letters from many of his English friends who were already in the war depressed him; his closest friend, Charles Norman, had already been a German prisoner of war for two years. "America has been infinitely saddened by the war," he wrote to Norman just before Christmas of 1916. "The thoughts of suffering Europe hang over us like a pall."[37] Early in February, 1917, Boyd left Doubleday and returned to Southern Pines; he planned to become somehow directly involved in the war.

IV   *The War*

Although Boyd's compassion for his English friends had kept him interested in the war since it began, his desire to become personally involved developed rather late. In a letter to his parents in August, 1914, he said he was relieved that fighting had not begun while he was at Cambridge because he would have found it difficult not to become involved, and yet would have lacked "the enthusiasm which comes from fighting for one's own country." He doubted that the United States would declare war; but, as the fighting continued, he sympathized more and more with England and France and wished fervently that the "detestable" Germans would get "the licking they deserve."[38] Later references to the war were confined wholly to the plight of England and France, however. Whatever the United States chose to do, Boyd came to feel, the immediate necessity was to assist England whose posture in the crisis was "more dignified and sane" than that of any other European country.

Boyd's illness and his general feeling of detachment prevented him from accompanying his brother, who joined a volunteer ambulance unit attached to the French army and participated in the Battle of Verdun in 1914; but James nevertheless kept up the artillery training he had begun in the artillery corps at Cambridge. He attended a National Guard artillery training camp at Tobyhanna, Pennsylvania, during the summer of 1915. In July, 1916, he enlisted as a private in the New York Artillery, but he was soon discharged by military doctors because of his physical condition. It was clear that he would never go on combat duty with the artillery.

When the United States finally entered the war in April, 1917, however, Boyd worked for several months with the Red Cross in New York, helping to solicit financial support for volunteer ambulance units. Finally, after persuading a New York doctor to operate on his sinuses, he applied for and received on August 28, 1917, a commission in the newly organized United States Army Ambulance Service. While he was waiting for orders, he became engaged to Katharine Lamont, daughter of Daniel Scott Lamont, who had been secretary and aide to Grover Cleveland during his first term as president and secretary of war during his second term. They were married in Millbrook, New York, on December 15, and went for their wedding trip to Southern Pines, where they stayed until Boyd's orders came late in February.

At Camp Crane, near Allentown, Pennsylvania, Boyd took command of Ambulance Service Section 520.[39] In May, orders came for thirty ambulance sections, including Section 520, to embark for Genoa, Italy. Each section supposedly consisted of twenty ambulances, forty-five men, and their commanding officer; but few had more than twelve ambulances and crews. The "ambulances" were slightly modified Model T Ford light trucks—with open cabs, high wooden-spoke wheels, wooden bodies, and canvas tops. In mid-June, the units moved out of New York Harbor, and by July 1, they had landed in Genoa.[40]

The ambulance units were attached to the 332nd Infantry Regiment of the Allied Expeditionary Force, assigned to the Italian front to "strengthen the morale" of the Italian army. For six weeks the regiment appeared briefly in various sectors "to create the impression that a large body of American troops had arrived." Whether or not such an impression was created, Lieutenant Boyd had severe reservations about the Italian army, which he later said was "in all respects, the most perfectly prepared army for every purpose—except fighting—the world has ever seen."[41]

Late in August, fifteen ambulance sections were transferred to France. Some went by rail, but Section 520 and eight others were driven overland from Genoa. The trip was spectacular—through the Piedmont to Turin, over the Alps and down to Modane, and on to Rimaucourt by way of Aix-les-Bains and Dijon. "Everything went splendidly," Boyd wrote to his wife: "The first night [we slept] on a Piedmont hilltop near an old farm built of immemorial stone. . . . The second half way up the Alps—hugging the shelf-like road in the bitter cold."[42] The ambulances reached Rimaucourt on September 4 and were sent immediately to the First Army Corps at Toul. "We crept along," Boyd wrote, "in the blackest of night without lights except for the winking fire of the guns stretching around us in a distant semi-circle."[43] Boyd's unit and the others assigned to the First Corps were to take part in the Saint-Mihiel operation, the first major engagement of the Allied Expeditionary Force.

At one o'clock in the morning of September 12, the Allied artillery began its barrage, and the infantry moved out four hours later. The ambulances, summoned from Norivant just as the drive started, transported men to the evacuation hospital south of Toul, a distance of approximately fifteen miles, crawling over roads nearly destroyed by bombardment and by a week of rain. After the battle the ambulances were sent for three days to Thiaucourt, one mile from the German lines, where they were shelled almost constantly Men were killed and ambulances destroyed in the section working next to Boyd's, but Section 520 was not damaged.[44]

When the Saint-Mihiel operation ended, preparations began immediately for the more massive Meuse-Argonne offensive. Boyd's section was assigned to the 35th Division, which was to lead the attack down the Aire River valley. The assault began through dense fog at dawn on September 25. Although hindered by bad weather and intense enemy artillery fire, the division took its towns on schedule and, before September 30, had reached its first-phase objective east of Apremont. During most of the battle, Ambulance Section 520 operated between the evacuation hospital at Neuvilly and the forward collection stations at Cheppy, Charpentry, and Varennes. Roads were so congested and the rain so heavy that a round trip from Cheppy to Neuvilly—about ten or twelve miles along the Aire River—took twenty-four hours.

In "Humoresque"—the only story Boyd based directly upon his war experience—the black emptiness predominates over every other impression during the operations of the ambulance units: "Nothing but blackness and the void ... through which the ambulances churned. ... They rocked, swung, and hung on to each other's tails like baby elephants lost in the African night."[45] But at least the darkness hid some of the carnage. At the Cheppy collection station at noon on September 29, nearly a thousand wounded men awaited treatment. Tents, buildings, and dugouts were jammed; three lines of men on litters stretched along the road for a hundred yards. In two hours, Boyd's section and one other moved seven-hundred and fifty men to Neuvilly.

Ambulance units remained at the front for one day after the division drew back to Varennes—long enough for Boyd to get caught in a bombardment of the Charpentry aid station that killed and wounded nearly eighty men. The incident was apparently still vividly etched in his memory when he wrote "Humoresque": "The stony path to the hospital seemed bleak and bare. The shells ... thumped and grunted in the open fields near by. ... Just ahead, a stone garden-house heaved up in a shower of fragments and black smoke."

After a brief lull during which Boyd's section rested at Rárécourt, the battle resumed September 31. Drivers worked in twenty-four-hour shifts, and ambulances ran as much as two hundred and eighty-eight hours without stopping.[46] But then the fighting ended abruptly, the Armistice was signed, and Boyd's ambulance section and others went to aid the sick and hungry people of Montmédy, a canton on the rocky slopes above the Chiers River, which had been occupied by the Germans for four years. "We have some 30 little villages & the town we are in," Boyd wrote to his wife. "You can stand on the old fort or one of the little cathedral towers & see the twisted red and gray slate roofs & beyond the gently sweeping hills & the soft olive colored fields & very dark hedgerows winding & winding beside the valley stream."[47]

After the muddled idealism of the war, the hills and fields and streams of Montmédy seemed real and solid. Like Frederick Henry in Hemingway's *A Farewell to Arms* ten years later, Boyd made a separate peace. The "most worthless bunch" in the war, he wrote to his wife, "are the chaplains [who] denounce the Germans as children of the Devil. . . . It is . . . worse than meaningless to me. . . . I have achieved the sublime mental & moral shif'lessness that is the key to happiness—when you try to talk to me of God & Satan & the Truth whatever they may be I reply by drawing a picture of a bear, which everyone knows what it is."[48]

On December 22, Boyd's unit was transferred out of the First Army, sent to Joinville, and subsequently to Sommermont. Three months later, after being confined to hospitals in Riaucourt, Paris, and London for treatment of his sinus condition, Boyd was shipped home. On July 2, 1919, his thirty-first birthday, he was discharged.

V Beyond the War

The war was the final step in Boyd's gradual move toward a literary career. From time to time during the war he had sent home poems with his letters, and he had apparently worked now and then on some stories.[49] Only two of the poems he wrote at this time survive, both in manuscript. One is about his Moore County friend James R. McConnell, an aviator in the Lafayette Escadrille:

> Flying for France, how often he looked down,
> To watch the clouds like icefields stretch away,
> And through the rifts saw many a ruined town,
> Where freemen held the enemy at bay.
>
> His airplane leaves the hangar now no more,
> No more he rides aloft upon the wind,
> But his brave soul forevermore shall soar
> For France—and for the freedom of mankind.[50]

The poem is badly flawed, but the image of "clouds like icefields" and the central metaphor are effective. Had the idealism been suggested through irony rather than hyperbole, the poem might have been successful. In a stanza of another lyric, Boyd did achieve an ironic effect, marred as it is by "purple" rhetoric:

> But let me never more taste victory
> Whose sharp aroma thrills my glowing heart,
> And sends my spirit soaring splendidly
> Ever so high, but lonely and apart,
> Up toward the very farthest stars to press,
> Ever to find a vaster emptiness.[51]

Boyd's response to the war, as his letters and these verses suggest, was midway between that of an older generation of writers whose complacency kept them from questioning the *status quo ante* and that of the writers ten years or so younger than himself, whose idealism—since it could not possibly become incarnate in a fallen world—resulted in disillusionment and expatriation. Boyd felt the attraction of the idealistic and uncomplicated past, but he recognized also the imperatives of the present and future. It was this doubleness of vision that was to give his writing much of its power.

By late in 1919, Boyd was committed to a literary career, and Southern Pines seemed to offer the best conditions for beginning —reasonable physical comfort, freedom from distractions, and mild climate. Shortly after Christmas, the Boyds moved south permanently—a move that was both a physical and an intellectual one. The choice of place was as significant as was Malcolm Cowley's and his friends' choice of Greenwich Village and Paris. As early as 1909, Boyd had remarked that "it is an unfortunate thing to become an expatriate. . . ."[52] Simultaneously, Southern Pines offered freedom from the stifling society of Harrisburg that he had rejected even before the war, and yet an opportunity to affirm the tangible values of American life. The attraction of Southern Pines was in one sense the same as that of Montmédy.

VI *Literary Apprenticeship*

In 1920, Southern Pines was still a bucolic village of seven hundred people, most of them farmers and farm workers. It seemed an inauspicious place for a writer to settle down, but Boyd was attracted to the relatively untouched freshness of the region even more intensely than he had been before he had decided to become a writer. In a sketch he soon wrote about a canoe trip down the Lumbee River, he evoked the primitive attractions of the landscape: "At High Hill we left the canoe and went home, thinking of the stream whose amber waters rise so darkly in the graveyard of lost ages and then flow on from where we left them, through the lands of the unsolved Croatans, through cypress, pine, cotton and rice, until at last under tropical festoons of hoary moss they join the sea."[53] During the next twenty-five years he explored the history, topography, and people of the region; and he discovered material for more than a dozen short stories and two novels. Southern Pines furnished him not only a vivid present but also a usable past.

Throughout the spring and summer of 1920 Boyd wrote stories steadily, having resolved to spend five years in a literary apprenticeship before he "either succeeded or gave up."[54] In midsummer he mailed two stories to Robert Bridges of *Scribner's Magazine*, who bought one of them, "The Sound of a Voice," for one hundred dollars. Boyd's first story actually to appear in print was "Old Pines," in *Century Magazine* for March, 1921. Others followed quickly; by 1925, he had published eleven stories in such magazines as *Scribner's, Century, Harper's* and the *Pictorial Review*.[55]

Although Boyd continued to publish stories for another twenty years, he had by about 1923 turned most of his attention to his first novel. He apparently had not intended to begin one so soon in his "apprenticeship"; but John Galsworthy, who was staying for some weeks in Moore County, had read some of his stories in manuscript, liked them, and encouraged Boyd to do so.[56]

VII   *The Novels*

By January, 1923, *Drums*, set during the American Revolution in North Carolina, was well under way. "The work is going better than I expected," Boyd told his Scribner's editor Maxwell Perkins, "but I am too green as yet to forecast even an approximate date of completion."[57] Early the next year the book was in type; after reading the galleys, Boyd decided it was a better story than he had thought but not as well written as he had hoped.[58] Far from being apologetic, Perkins felt that it was with Boyd and other young authors that the "great hopes" of Scribner's lay. "We know what the old authors can do and,

although some of them do admirably, they seldom surprise us,"
he said. "But the young writers may do anything—at least several of them may, and you are certainly one of those several."[59]

After *Drums* was released March 27, 1925, it went through
four printings in one month; virtually all reviewers agreed with
E. C. Beckwith of the New York *Evening Post* that it was "the
finest novel of the American Revolution which has yet been
written."[60] Sales ran to five thousand copies a month for eight
months; by the end of the year, sales totaled more than fifty
thousand copies.[61] John Galsworthy thought it as excellent a
first novel as had ever been written.[62]

Months before *Drums* was in print, Boyd began a novel
about the Civil War in the South. For his materials he went
not only to the archives but to the land itself, traveling all over
the state for weeks with his friend Paul Green, stopping to talk
with farmers in the fields, country storekeepers, and somnolent
sages tilted back in their split-bottom chairs against the faded
fronts of village filling stations. *Marching On*, which was completed late in 1926, went on sale in the spring of 1927. Although
it was a greater popular success than *Drums* (sales were nearly
eighty thousand the first year), it was not received as well
critically. James Southall Wilson, who gave it one of its most
perceptive reviews, found it inferior in some ways to the first
novel but still "worthy of the author of *Drums*."[63]

Boyd apparently contemplated a third war novel, but he decided instead to write of the trans-Appalachian frontier. When
Long Hunt was finished, he felt it was the best of his novels
so far;[64] but, paradoxically, his audience was dwindling. The
period of his greatest public acclaim had passed with *Marching
On*. Reviewers praised *Long Hunt* rather warmly, but sales
during the first months were barely half what they had been for
Drums and *Marching On*.

In the fall of 1930 Boyd started his fourth novel, hoping to
finish it in about two years; but a series of sinus operations intervened, and it did not appear until 1935. "I have been fighting
sinus trouble and a novel all winter long," he told a friend early
in 1932, "until I can't tell which is producing which."[65]

Book I of *Roll River*, called "Dark Shore," was first published serially in *Scribner's Magazine* beginning in May, 1934;
it ran concurrently with Fitzgerald's *Tender Is the Night*. Critical
reception of the novel was good, but again sales lagged. Boyd's

disappointment was only slightly compensated by the fact that the North Carolina Literary and Historical Association gave *Roll River* its Mayflower Award for the best book by a North Carolinian, belatedly acknowledging that Boyd had, as Jonathan Daniels was to note later, "given North Carolina a literature" before it had one of its own.[66]

Boyd was slow in beginning his next novel, which was to be set in the Wyoming cattle country at the end of the nineteenth century. Illness and interruptions came so frequently that *Bitter Creek* did not go on sale until March, 1939.[67] Compared to *Roll River*, it sold well—thirteen thousand copies the first month; but it remains his weakest novel, nevertheless. With *Bitter Creek*, Boyd's career as a novelist ended. It had begun with enormous public acclaim—acclaim that waned and was partially compensated for by "official" recognition. In 1937, he was elected to the National Institute of Arts and Letters; in 1938, he received an honorary doctorate from the University of North Carolina; and in 1939, he was elected to the new Society of American Historians, along with Henry Steele Commager, Carl Van Doren, Allan Nevins, and others. Boyd accepted the honors with diffident grace. A "synthetic pundit," he called himself upon receiving the honorary degree, "a Kentucky colonel among the West Pointers of profundity."

VIII *The Later Years*

In late 1939, there was little doubt that a second world war was far away, or that the United States would be a part of it when it came. Having seen the Allied Expeditionary Force in operation in France twenty years earlier and having watched the development of the United States' military machine during the 1930's, Boyd felt that the country was technologically prepared for war. But he feared that the shock of war when it came might lead the nation psychologically on a course of resigned despair, cynical isolationism, or blind Fascistic vengeance.

Boyd's faith in the essential integrity of the common man, however, gave him confidence that American writers might provide the needed direction if they could be heard by enough of the common people. In the fall of 1940 he organized a group of writers—including Archibald MacLeish, Sherwood Anderson, Stephen Vincent Benét, Paul Green, Elmer Rice, William Saroyan,

and others—into the Free Company of Players. During the
winter and spring of 1941, the Free Company broadcast plays
about the meaning of democracy to a radio audience of nearly
five million persons each week, demonstrating in the process that
writers could direct their attention specifically to the defense
of national ideals without necessarily sacrificing their artistic
integrity.[68]

Such activity left little time for writing, and Boyd's health
was progressively deteriorating, despite repeated operations
on his sinuses. His last short story had appeared in 1937 and his
last novel in 1939. As the war continued, he returned to poetry,
of which he had written little since World War I. His poems
began to appear in *Harper's*, the *Atlantic Monthly*, and elsewhere. Many had a common theme—the war and its effect on
the human spirit: "Song for the Silent," "Now That the Clouds
of War," "Casualty," "Civilian Night Song," and others.[69] There
was little in the poems of the practice of the New Poets and
their successors, either in theme or technique; for Boyd's intention was simply to express in poetry his own mature vision.
"It is slow hard work," he told Paul Green, "and of course utterly
unprofitable, but I must say uniquely satisfying."[70] Among the
fewer than two dozen poems Boyd wrote, three are unquestion-
ably the best: "Love Still Has Something," a sonnet whose
delicate imagery suggests the unity of sexual and chthonian
rhythms; "Answer, Sky," a six-stanza lyric which affirms the
paradoxical "singing" in man's blood amid the terrors of his
experience; and "Echoes of Earth,"[71] probably the last poem
he wrote.

As a unifying theme and narrative bridge, "Echoes of Earth"
employs the refrain:

> *The sky and sea speak loud,*
> *But the earth speaks clear.*
> *Put an ear to the ground.*
> *Listen. You will hear.*

The echoes are those not only of natural rhythms but also of the
common historical experience of mankind:

> Under my heart, now, I can feel a beating,
> A pulse, not mine; profounder than my own,
> As though earth had a heart which kept repeating,
> In time with mine, a tale it must make known.

> There are no words to that deep murmuring,
> But, as a shell holds echoes of the sea,
> Earth echoes bygone steps; their tramp and swing
> March in the pulse that marches now to me. . . .

The "bygone steps" are those of a column of marchers who stretch back through space and time to the beginnings of the national experience, and whose steps echo and reecho: "deerhide moccasin and wooden shoe," "varnished British boot," "Indian ponies' barefoot tread," and "broad black feet, unfree, unshod." Intermittently comes the refrain, both as warning against easy certainty and as promise in despair: *"Put an ear to the ground./ Listen. Can you hear?"* The poem ends in a guarded affirmation:

> I touch the ground in sign that I have heard.
> Old earth, I need no more from you to me;
> My heart is marching to your steady word;
> I stand up now to face the sky and sea.
>
> I do not know the ending to this day
> Or how much of our hope is lost or won,
> But trust that at the end I, too, can say
> To the unborn who follow:

> *Daughter . . . Son,*
> *The sky and sea speak loud,*
> *But the earth speaks clear.*
> *Put an ear to the ground.*
> *Listen. You will hear.*

On February 25, 1944, Boyd died while at Princeton University to speak at a training school for British army officers.

IX *Boyd's Mind and the Paradoxes of His Career*

When Sherwood Anderson met James Boyd at Paul Green's home in Chapel Hill, North Carolina, on a December evening in 1936, Anderson was surprised to discover that Boyd, who seemed to be a "true artist," lived "among the rich" in a resort town and was passionately fond of horses and fox-hunting. During the evening, Boyd told Anderson that Thomas Wolfe, who had recently visited him while he was in the hospital in New York, had sat on the side of Boyd's bed and declaimed loudly that Sherwood Anderson was "the only man in America who ever taught me anything." The story as Boyd told it, Anderson said, "gave me new courage, a thing rather needed just now. . . ."[72]

Two months later Anderson was still puzzled about Boyd. "So here is this man," he told Maxwell Perkins, "rich, with a big estate, a huge pack of fox-hounds, the sort of people about who go in for fox-hunting, all rich, decked out in their white pants and red coats, going whooping and tearing across the country, over fences, the whole thing seeming in some way so absurd just now, so far away from anything that matters, and yet Jim himself with such a sincere love of horses and dogs and, I'm sure, with a fine mind."[73] Anderson's response to Boyd reveals something about the assumptions writers in America have frequently shared concerning the *authentic* creative personality.

Perhaps more often than not, American writers have defined themselves in romantic terms. In the 1930's, of course, Thomas Wolfe was a prime example. What perplexed Anderson was that Wolfe's praise had come by way of James Boyd, who neither acted entirely as the artist in America is supposed to act nor lived as the artist is supposed to live—as did Wolfe, Fitzgerald, or Hemingway. The artist may go to transact "private business" with himself at Walden Pond, hunt big game in Africa, or tramp ten thousand streets in search of "a stone, a leaf, a door"; but he may not establish himself in country-squire fashion and ride to hounds unless he does not mind having his artistic credentials checked from time to time.

The fact is that both Boyd's mind and his way of life were in many respects strikingly atypical of American writers in the 1920's and 1930's. He had not been an expatriate; he had served only a short apprenticeship as a newspaper reporter; when he decided on a literary career, he had settled not in Greenwich Village or in Westchester County but in Moore County, North Carolina; he had neither divorces nor mistresses; and his life was always more private than public. Sherwood Anderson was responding essentially to the paradoxes created by these facts and others, in conjunction with Boyd's personality and the events of his highly successful literary career. How could Boyd roam the country in worn tweed one day, looking for materials for novels and stories, and be dressed in an impeccable riding habit the next? How could he be both liberal *and* conservative? Both a northerner and a southerner? An intellectual and not an intellectual? An artist and not an artist?

If we look carefully at Boyd's major ideas and examine their relationship to certain events in his later career, we discover that many of the paradoxes are resolved. Interestingly enough, Boyd's last poem suggests the four dominant strains of his thought. In the first place, he was committed to what Rebecca West has called living "outward from the center." For him, that center was the South, which offered a kind of stability. The metaphor of "Echoes of Earth" is dynamic in every respect, however; what he hears with his "ear to the ground" suggests not stasis but change and movement. That such dynamism is not only inevitable but also the source of constantly renewed hope is the second major idea that may be observed in Boyd's writing. He also had a radical, although by no means uncritical, faith in democracy, both in concept and in practice. Finally, he had a strong historical sense—a sense, as T. S. Eliot phrased it, "not only of the pastness of the past, but of its presence." An exploration of these four major aspects of Boyd's thought may prove useful as a conclusion to this brief account of his life.

THE SOUTH. Boyd's living in the South and his writing about it were closely related. When he moved to Southern Pines in 1920, the New South was fast becoming an accomplished fact, but remnants of the social patterns of the Old South remained; and Boyd identified himself in some senses with them both. In his stories and novels, the New South represents the only viable ideal; but the Old South remains as a way of life that had at least an esthetic appeal.

Boyd himself was wealthy, and his life in Southern Pines was in many senses aristocratic. In his position as master of the Moore County Hounds he represented an insoluble enigma to Sherwood Anderson. From early November until the season ended in February—as many as sixty times in a season—Boyd rode to hounds. He maintained a small stable of horses and a pack of hounds, and he once estimated that starting a modest pack would cost at least six thousand dollars, and half as much every year to maintain.[74] As a result, most hunts in the United States were composed of wealthy people who could afford the expensive equipment and clothing required. As such, it was a relic of a condition of society that no longer existed; but for

Boyd it filled persistent human needs, and to that extent it was alive and relevant.

Although fox-hunters frequently make arthritic attempts to defend the expense and danger of hunting on the pseudomoral grounds that it engenders courage, resourcefulness, and love of God and mankind, Boyd admitted that the posture was needless: "It would be not only simpler to say that people hunt for fun; that they squander money; catch cold; desert their wives; break their necks; get robbed by dealers; . . . wear tight boots in the cold weather . . . it would be not only simpler to say this,— it would also do more honor to the sport."[75]

Boyd's candor is attractive, but it does not reveal the complex emotional and esthetic attractions of the sport:

the feel of a horse's lifting shoulders, the swing of hounds across the grass, the sweep of a hunting country. . . . These things are among the beauties of this earth; and they are reinforced by a thousand minor joys . . . by the quality of leather and melton and cord, by soft, late-August day-breaks and hard, bright mornings of November. . . . But I think there must be something deeper. . . . From their Olympian height [fox-hunters] witness a drama of life and death . . . in which quest, discovery, surprise, pursuit, blind chance, skill, escape and doom mingle . . . a drama which they themselves have initiated . . . but which, once launched, they cannot control. . . .[76]

CHANGE AS A CONDITION OF LIFE. As attractive as Boyd found the lingering charm of the institutions of the Old South, he knew almost to the point of revulsion and hatred that it had to change. In Atlanta "they've indicted 2 niggers 2 white men & 2 girls for a capital offense, inciting insurrection, because they held an unemployment meeting," he wrote to a friend at the depth of the depression. "Altogether it takes quite a little forgiving this fair land of ours, & I can't say I'm up to it."[77] In the absence of the deluge of civil-rights legislation that was still three decades in the future, Boyd realized that necessary change would have to come town by town and county by county. Southern Pines and Moore County he made his own area of responsibility, and he repeatedly showed himself to be an effective exponent of social change, especially in the area of Negro rights.

In the early 1930's, Southern Pines annexed "Jimtown," the Negro section adjacent to it. Boyd favored the annexation because as a separate municipality Jimtown (officially, West Southern Pines) had been subject to exploitation by unscrupulous businessmen and its own elected officials. Boyd was dismayed to discover later that the annexation was viewed in some northern periodicals as a cynical attempt by whites to take advantage of the Negroes. An editorial in the New York *Dunbar News* implied that a village of respectable colored servants and workmen, previously governed in a model way by their own officials, had without due process been deprived of their legitimate rights and property. In a carefully documented letter to William Jay Schieffelin of the New York Citizens Union, Boyd demonstrated that West Southern Pines was in fact a self-governing ghetto in which streets were impassable and unlighted, fire protection impossible, sewage-disposal facilities unavailable, crime rampant, and taxes neither honestly collected nor expended. Since annexation, Boyd showed, a water main had been installed and streets were being improved, even though such improvements would cost Southern Pines more than increased tax revenues would bring in. Even such changes, Boyd admitted, were of limited efficacy since they merely improved the Negroes' living conditions temporarily and did not touch the problem of social, economic, and political development.[78]

Some years later, taking issue with Negro intellectuals who had attacked white southern liberals, Boyd suggested that of the two general strategies available to Negroes in their quest for social justice—gradualism and violence—the latter was less likely to succed in the long run.[79] Citing the Civil War as the only major "departure from gradualism" in the United States' internal affairs, one that finally produced not what the Negro most needed but "only the bare abolition of chattel servitude," Boyd insisted that current efforts should be concentrated on the economic front, where "the enemy is weakest... [and] the Negro's friends are most numerous." If violence could really advance the Negro's cause, he concluded, Negroes would be "justified in denouncing those who counsel moderation." But not only would violence not bring lasting change, it would likely destroy the saving attributes of the Negro personality that had borne him up thus far. Of all "substitutes for justice," he said, "sentimentality is the most offensive"; but a recognition of those attributes was at the moment a strategic imperative.[80]

The most effective instrument Boyd himself used to help

bring about the broad, fundamental change he espoused was the Southern Pines *Pilot,* which he bought in 1941, soon after the Free Company series ended. Founded in nearby Vass in 1920, the *Pilot* had never been more than a tottering local weekly, distinguished chiefly for its indulgent provincialism and conservative editorials. In 1923, citing the "great principle of 'America for Americans,' " it hailed a Supreme Court ruling that Japanese could not become United States citizens as "assurance that yellow will never threaten white supremacy in these lands." The paper was nearly bankrupt and its equipment was antiquated when Boyd bought it. "I do not expect to get anything much for myself out of the Pilot," he said, "beyond the satisfaction of giving the town a good paper."[81] By purchasing new equipment, expanding circulation, and taking a liberal editorial stance, Boyd transformed the paper. For the first time, the *Pilot* began to receive awards from the North Carolina Press Association.[82]

DEMOCRATIC ARISTOCRAT. The blend of the aristocratic sensibility and democratic ideas we find in Boyd has recurred consistently in American history—most notably and productively, perhaps, in eighteenth-century Virginia. The aristocratic aspects of his life Boyd enjoyed and found little fault with, but his ideas were radically democratic.[83] Even the traditionally aristocratic sport of hunting he saw in essentially democratic terms. The hunt should "belong to the town," he said, and no one who was seriously interested in hunting should ever be refused a place, whether he could afford to dress properly or not. "I don't want to discourage the farmers from coming out," he had told Charles Norman as early as 1916, even though, with farmers on horses more accustomed to pulling wagons than jumping fences, the hunt was frequently somewhat comical. "We laid hounds on and off we went," Boyd said of one New Year's hunt. "When we struck the first fence it sounded like the collapse of The Crystal Palace. I looked back [and] there was a cloud of smoke & flying timbers & when the air cleared the fence was gone but all the field were on the right side & riding to beat hell."[84]

To Boyd, democracy was, almost in the eighteenth-century sense, a mirror held up to man's very nature—not simply the most congenial one of a number of competing political ideologies. "The belief that leads to democracy," he said, "is . . . that every man has something sacred about him. This sacredness is held to be inherent and perpetual: no rules, no religion, no group of men, no government is justified in violating it. It is the first principle of a man's life and nothing takes precedence over it. . . ."[85] The vision of a democratic society that guaranteed the dignity of the human personality, Boyd said, had the power of "eternal self-renewal."

Boyd's democratic liberalism had its limits, however. Although he was a regular contributor for years to the American Civil Liberties Union, he refused to support various kinds of political and ideological cant that masqueraded as liberalism in the 1930's. When he was approached through the Union in 1934 for a donation to the Tom Mooney Defense Committee, he objected strongly to the caption on the brochure: "Labor's Champion—a Class War Prisoner—for 18 Years the Victim of a Monstrous Capitalistic Class Frame-Up." Boyd protested to Director Roger Baldwin that the caption would make his contribution "an endorsement of Communism."[86] Boyd was willing to help not only Mooney but also the Americans whose Nazi sympathies had recently been defended by the American Civil Liberties Union, but he was not willing to have his contribution taken as an endorsement of either Communist or Nazi ideology.

Boyd was aware of the failures and abuses of laissez-faire capitalism, but he distinguished between the capitalistic and the democratic aspects of the American experiment in a way that was all too uncommon in the 1930's. There was a quality of balance about his mind that saved him from the ideological shortsightedness of some of his contemporaries. To him, the issues of the American Civil Liberties Union incident in particular and of the 1930's in general were not greatly different from those of the 1860's or the 1780's. As such, they were not to be solved by uncritical endorsement of modish ideologies.

THE SENSE OF HISTORY. Boyd characteristically took the long view of human experience. To him, man was first of all a creature of history whose problems had to be understood in historical depth. Herein lies the enduring relevance of Boyd's work. On the one hand he understood and found drama in the present human condition that has always been the primary domain of the literary artist; at one level, the value of his short stories and novels is independent of any actual or supposed historical qualities. On the other hand, his historical sense—besides in many ways governing his choice of material—allowed his writings to comment on the human condition and more particularly on the American experience, with a depth frequently denied to artists who lack that sense.

The tragedy of Hemingway's Jake Barnes in *The Sun Also Rises*, for instance, is valid in its own terms; but Barnes's historical isolation robs his tragedy of the broader validity it might otherwise have had. In comparison with the serenity of his friend the Count Mippipopolous, who has at least a rudimentary historical sense, Barnes's anxiety and isolation seem less than absolutely necessary. An even better example is the Count Greffi in Hemingway's *A Farewell to Arms*. And of course Robert Jordan's historical consciousness is one reason that Hemingway's *For Whom the Bell Tolls* has a breadth that neither *The Sun Also Rises* nor *A Farewell to Arms* has.[87]

To carry the argument one step further, it might be maintained that novels of the 1920's and 1930's that now appear dated or limited in statement appear so partly because their protagonists have no sense of their place in history. Their tragedies are those of men who find themselves "strangers and afraid" in a world not of their own making, in a world, that is, whose history—and therefore whose meaning and order—they do not know. Not knowing it, they assume it has none, which defines the very conditions of their fear and anxiety. Whether such a state of mind was itself a broad characteristic of American experience in the 1930's is a compelling question that is unfortunately beyond the scope of this book.

The argument here is limited to the assertion that although Boyd's protagonists may be, and often are, afraid, they are rarely strangers in the world because they know how it came to be. The dichotomy between novels that are confined to the present and those whose awareness of the present is sharpened by a sense of history suggests, in fact, the critical plan of this study.

CHAPTER 2

Learning the Craft: The Short Stories

B OYD always referred to the first few years of his career as an "apprenticeship," and he entitled his first published comments on writing "Learning the Craft."[1] In a letter to a Princeton undergraduate in 1922, he called writing a "trade" that could be learned by "any man who has the comparatively small invention needed to construct plots and the tireless devotion required to secure some slight mastery of language." Some allowance must be made for the fact that Boyd was trying to assure an aspiring young writer that one who had no discernible "genius" might still hope to write effectively, but the Horatian flavor of the statement is clear. His own first published story, he said in "Learning the Craft," was simply "a study in character with particular effort to achieve good style." The implication was that both character portrayal and style could be learned and perfected through practice, much as the elements of cabinet-making might have been learned by an apprentice in the eighteenth century.

Because of such an approach, it is not surprising that Boyd's early stories are quite varied. One learns to write, after all, by consciously practicing each separate aspect of the craft—character, setting, dialogue, action, tone, and so forth. The stories range from the commonplace setting and bitter tone of "Bars" to the remote, almost Gothic setting and elegiac tone of "Out of the Mist"; from the Romantic themes of "The Sound of a Voice" to the Naturalistic ones of "Uan the Fey"; from the florid style of "The Verse on the Window" to the stark, Hemingwayesque "Fiesta." Taken together, however, the stories show considerable unity in subject and theme,[2] despite their experimental origins. Most of them are concerned essentially with either the beauty and ugliness of the life and mind of the South or with the radical vulnerability of the artist in a conservative, materialistic society. Preoccupation with the South dominates the early stories, and the artist's problems the stories of the 1930's; but both concerns are present all along.

I *Stories of the Artist and Society*

Although Boyd's own artistic practice rested upon Neo-classical principles of conscious craftsmanship, the artists in his stories are defined in fundamentally Romantic terms. Several of the earliest stories deal with the artist's attempt to achieve the state of heightened sensitivity commonly assumed by the Romantic to precede artistic creation.[3]

The protagonist of "The Sound of a Voice,"[4] Roger Pender, is an architect by trade but an artist by inclination. Watching a lavishly staged and insensitively acted historical drama, he feels only disgust at its bathos until the voice of a young girl who is playing a minor role arrests his attention. When he manages to meet her, he discovers that in her company he is able to see "new beauty" in his usually dull routine; he exults in a new love "of all of life and her." When Eile Darragh—the name itself is Romantic—suddenly disappears, Pender wanders gloomily through the streets searching for her. He chances upon a marionette theater, whose tiny figures, he notes bitterly, seem "absurdly human." But from behind the stage he hears Eile's voice, her only remaining theatrical asset since her face has been scarred in an accident; its sound fills him again with "undreamed hopes and powers." The theme is familiar: innate poetic sensitivity, dulled by monotonous routine, may be stirred to life again by love, which alone purifies life and gives it beauty and meaning.

The theme is repeated with a more conventional subject and setting in "The Verse on the Window."[5] Weatherby Heath, a writer whose aspirations far exceed his meager attainments, discovers in a dilapidated country inn a beautiful tinted window that is inscribed with a Romantic quatrain. As the current owner of the tavern tells him the story of the young cavalier who cut the inscription with his diamond ring (and subsequently lost his life at the hands of the outraged innkeeper), Heath recalls a moment in his own past when, inspired by a vision of his beloved, he was able to write a beautiful sonnet. Boyd arranges, through a skillful use of outdated but still effective Gothic machinery (apparitions, disembodied voices), for Heath to encounter the martyred young poet, whose "last blazing moment of defiance" he sees both as a reproach to his own failure and as a potential source of renewed inspiration. "The Verse on the Window" employs many of the motifs of "The Sound of a Voice," but it makes more explicit the problems the artist faces: clouded vision, spiritual aridity, self-doubt, and failure of will.

The problem of self-doubt is further explored in another of the early stories, "The Superman."[6] By presenting its theme from an ironic point of view, it avoids the bathos that mars both "The Sound of a Voice" and "The Verse on the Window." Wilton Durand, who fancies himself an artist and an intellectual, edits a pseudo-Nietzschean art magazine, *The Superman*. He rationalizes its eventual failure as a result not of his own ineptitude but of the lack of an audience sophisticated enough to appreciate its profundity. Durand's superhuman talent is appreciated only by his wife, who unfortunately seems to lack other signs of intelligence. When she graciously slides a tea tray onto the table before him, a pile of books is pushed off, and he sneers: "As Sir Isaac Newton has so justly observed . . . all actions and reactions are equal. A square foot of tea replaces a square foot of art. Life is a compromise." Searching for a job to match his talents, Durand is finally hired as a drama critic for a newspaper. In a surprising flashback at the end of the story, his wife is seen persuading the editor to hire her husband. The effect of the story derives from the ironic tension between the weakness and bitter arrogance of Durand and the compassion and quiet strength of his wife.

Two early stories that have the artist as their subject were considered by Boyd as experiments in the use of setting to produce a predetermined effect. One of them, "Out of the Mist,"[7] is not successful, primarily because the remote and fantastic North Sea island setting requires too great a suspension of disbelief. But Boyd was still convinced that the setting had possibilities; he planned to trace—in a series of five stories—the family history of the Shanes, Druidic tribal artisans who inhabited a similar mystical island. Of the three stories that he actually wrote, only one, "Uan the Fey," was published.[8]

The Shane family is a venerable one; when a Shane dies, he is "buried with all the ancient Shanes, strong men and mighty

builders, who lay inside the great stone ring at Kroona."[9] Beard-
less Uan Shane, "the practical artist neither understood nor
admired" in his village,[10] is different from the bearded Shanes
who have gone before; their epic quest for power, symbolized
by their massive architectural works, interests him not at all:
"Instead of their incoherent fury for work, a flame of joy in
making things burned in his heart, its smoke a curling wisp of
quizzical fancy, its ashes God knows what lost visions of ease
and comfort. This was to be a builder before whose dreams-
come-true the works of the bearded Shanes would be lifeless
things. . . ."[11]

Uan's passion for the delicately beautiful leads him to paint
a temple mural, considered by the village elders to be profane.
So great is the elders' anger that they murder Uan; then, in
grotesque ritual, they form a column, "moving their goat-skin
sandals with a sifting sound." One of them begins a chant, and
they lift Uan's body on their shoulders: "The chant rose a note
. . . [and] they moved forward with their burden. . . . Their song
rang and quivered for a moment . . . and then was drowned in
the hoarse, full-throated wolf-scream of the city mob."

After "Uan the Fey," Boyd moved away from exotic settings,
but he retained some of the Naturalistic motifs he had discovered there. In doing so, he wrote his best stories of the artist
in society. "Bars,"[12] the most successful of them, except perhaps for "The Flat Town," has as its protagonist not a Romantic,
ineffectual poet, but a cynical young burglar who takes esthetic
pride in his work. He cares for the "nest of bright steel" in his
burglar's satchel as a sculptor might care for his chisels. At a
New York zoo he watches bitterly as the animals slide "like long
buff shuttles, to and fro, weaving the endless texture of their
despair." One leopard intrigues him especially; refusing to
accept its own captivity, it stays "withdrawn in pride and hatred."

When the young man is soon caught trying to break into a
building at night, he is himself imprisoned. As the months
pass, he feels his spirit die—"dead as the dripping stones and
ringing steel. . . dead as the strip of chill, indifferent sky" outside
his cell window. When he is at last paroled, he returns to the
zoo and finds the leopard still with its "yellow eyes . . . straight
ahead, fixed perhaps on some distant horizon where he saw the
ice-sheets and fir-trees of his mountain home." Unable to bear
the existential paradox any longer, the young man slips into the

zoo at night and uses his burglar's skill to free the leopard, cele-
brating the act with a "long, fierce, mocking prison cry." A
guard shoots him as he flees; and, as he dies, he gives a "cough-
ing laugh" and rolls over on his back, "staring at the stars."

The idea of the craftsman as artist was also explored in
"Luck,"[13] the story of a tower builder who tries to defy the
physical laws of the universe in a search for perfection in his
work. But he slips from a tower and is killed, and his spirtual
quest is inherently limited by the laws of physical reality. It is
Ishmael's dilemma on the masthead again. In a sense, "Luck"
was a sketch for "The Flat Town,"[14] which employs some of
the same motifs and themes but treats them more successfully.
In "The Flat Town," the tower builders defy not the physical
laws of the universe but the social and moral conventions of a
small town. The monotonous regularity of the "straight, parallel
equidistant" streets in Central Junction is a metaphor for the
pale uniformity of its citizens, whose individuality is marked
only by "imperceptibly fine shades of relative obscurity." The
deathly order of the "primitive tribal village" is enforced by
Wilmer Scabes: "It was, he often said, good enough for him.
And neither he . . . nor his ring of moon-faced auditors caught
. . . the dreadful implication."

Scabes rules "with the heavy power of his righteousness"
until "three pagan mechanics" arrive to build a new town water
tower. The tower rises, and the spirits of the workmen rise with
it. Lifted above the pious spiritual flatness of the town, they
shout scandalous but rhapsodic oaths toward the heavens. With
"a double syncopated accompaniment" of pneumatic rivet ham-
mers, they sing bawdy ballads in a pagan celebration of sensual-
ity: "O-o-o-o-o-h . . . She-e-e-e ripped and she snorted and she
rolled on the floor—." Scabes feels bound to "bring the three
pagan mechanics to a conviction of sin," but he discovers that
their ribald evening song has inexplicably become for him "a
sort of diabolic angelus."

One evening the "black and shapeless figure" of Scabes slowly
ascends the tower in a final attempt to silence the workmen.
As he gains the top, however, the workmen "point across the
plain into the blazing West where the Blue Ridge rose, then
eastward toward the sea, hid from the groundlings under the
shoulder of the world." Unable to speak, Scabes can only stare
"into the heart of the distant light." As the workers sing again,

he stands "rapt and radiant, gazing into the eye of the sinking sun, gently swaying to the rhythm of their song."

Taken as a group, Boyd's stories about the artist suggest that society does not foster or appreciate art or the artist; it fears, distrusts, and seeks to expel him. Conversely, the artist understands his own values and commitments to be antithetical to those of society. His role is fraught with unavoidable peril: failure of the will, failure to create during the brief and relatively infrequent periods when creation is possible, and failure to appreciate the ironic fact that the vision that fits him for his career makes him vulnerable in practical matters and, therefore, subject to delusion about his own abilities and easy prey for a hostile society. The artist is paradoxically the victim of his own special competence.

Both the esthetic and the world view of the stories are dual. One creates works of art only by conscious craftsmanship, but the energy to produce comes solely from inspiration. The *existence* of the work of art comes from the interplay of the mind, the will, and the hands with reality, but its *essence* derives from the spirit's engagement with the ideal. The esthetic is paralleled in every respect by the world view. Virtually every protagonist in the stories of the artist is motivated by a belief that ideals do exist, that they are worthy of pursuit, and that the perfect work of art gives substance and objective existence to them.

On the other hand, the antithesis between the artist and society is only symptomatic of a larger antithesis implied by the narrative point of view of the better stories. The artist may proclaim both to society and to the universe, "Sir, I exist!"; but his proclamation does not create in the universe a "sense of obligation" to honor or protect his ideals. The stories suggest increasingly that the universe is Naturalistic—it is therefore at least "flatly indifferent," if not actually hostile, to his ideal strivings. But the strivings remain, because they arise from irreducible human needs, as Joseph Wood Krutch has suggested in *The Modern Temper* (1929). "Bars" establishes the limit of Boyd's excursion into Naturalistic bitterness in the stories, but the motif was present in virtually all of them. Even the Romantic protagonist of "The Sound of a Voice," we recall, watches the "absurdly human" antics of the marionettes and wonders whether "his own frantic wanderings so appeared to the deity who watched the world from some celestial lobby; assuming, of course, that they were observed at all."[15]

The problem Boyd faced as he developed as a writer was in one sense the problem of his protagonists: how to reconcile ideal values with a Naturalistic world view. In the earliest stories, no believable reconciliation occurs. The result is a great deal of sentimentality and more than a little bathos. Later, as the subjects allowed (and in a few cases almost forced) the Naturalistic world view to control the tone of the stories, results improved markedly. In the best of the stories—"Uan the Fey," "Bars," "The Flat Town"—there is genuine pathos, irony, and a sense of the inescapable contradictions that are the basis not only of art but of life itself.

Boyd was unable, however, to respond completely to the stylistic implications of a Naturalistic world view. Frequently, for instance, a genteel decorum prevented his exploring in sufficient detail the depravity of his characters. In "The Flat Town," the beginning of the bawdy ballad is quoted; but we are then told that the riveters sang "right on through to the outrageous and unspeakable climax." The insistent Freudian possibilities of images are only rarely and obliquely implied. Boyd may have been restrained by the genteel sensibilities of his editors (he was publishing in the more genteel magazines), but his stature as a writer in the mid- and late 1920's would have guaranteed publication elsewhere (for example, in the *American Mercury*, which published his "Civic Crisis" in 1937) if he had chosen. The fact is that he did not so choose. A somewhat tedious delicacy can be a virtue if it is organically related to theme and point of view, but such was rarely the case in the stories.

We notice finally that the early stories which employ regional subjects and settings are generally superior to those that do not. One reason "The Flat Town" is so successful is that its setting is a metaphor for a state of mind. The resulting dramatic and thematic unity is far superior to that of any of the other artist stories. To put it another way, Boyd found, after many experiments, the place where his stories "happened" best: the South.[16] Of the eleven stories Boyd published before 1925, only three have southern settings; of the nine published between 1925 and 1944, seven are southern. The big-city settings of the very early stories and the mythical ones of the Shane stories were gradually displaced by the small-town, mid-South settings that always proved more fruitful. It is not surprising that, although only two of the eight artist stories are really first rate, all of the stories of the South are excellent.

II   *Stories of the South*

"Old Pines,"[17] Boyd's first published story, remains one of his best. He modestly described it, as we have noted, as "a study in character with particular effort to achieve good style"; but it is more than that. It is a study in the character of an entire region at a crucial point in its history: "Old man McDonald sat in the house of his ancestors watching his little railroad die. Its wabbling single track left the Great Southern . . . and, climbing with laborious eccentricity, passed near the composed and graceful portico . . . and meandered away through a ragged wilderness toward the vanished glories of an abandoned port."[18]

Twice McDonald has built his railroad, and twice he has watched it die. The land it runs through was once covered by magnificent virgin pine forests, and the railroad prospered by carrying turpentine from them to the sea. When the supply and most of the demand for turpentine have gone, the road withers away. Then the ancient trees themselves are felled, and the railroad hauls them away. At the time of the story, McDonald is trying to resist the offer of a Yankee sharpster who wants to buy the railroad as "junk" in order to take advantage of an industrial boom McDonald does not know is impending.

McDonald's personal tragedy suggests the complex agony of an agrarian society trying to preserve itself in an increasingly industrial economy. In a way that is now familiar to readers of Faulkner and of the Agrarians (especially John Crowe Ransom, Allen Tate, and Donald Davidson), McDonald's tragedy cannot be separated from the history of the land. The very character of the land provides his sense of identity. The song of the Negroes who help him build the railroad—"a song which had come from forests of mangrove and ebony"—echoes down "aisles of cypress and pine" and makes him vaguely aware of his niche in the historical and ecological scheme of things, represented metaphorically by the land itself.

The basic paradox is that the energy and sense of purpose

McDonald gains from the land is used to destroy it. Having drained the vital juices of the pines and having felled trees themselves, McDonald is haunted by a vision of "branches of great pines . . . old pines that were no more, come back to see his fall." His guilt is as inescapable as his choice was inevitable; such a system cannot sustain itself without spending the capital that not only allowed it to exist but also gave its existence meaning. In despair, McDonald looks "across the waste lands" now covered with "useless scrub oaks [standing] in puny triumph over the old masters."

McDonald's awareness of the implications of his failure is limited, but its implications are fully explored in the story. Clearly, the land cannot remain in its virgin state; the pressures of civilization are too great. Whether man's changing of the land is defensible in human terms depends upon his attitude toward the work of transformation. Of the three basic attitudes in the story, the least respectable is that of the sharpster Weiler, one of the "hard-faced men" of the North who "loved business dealing as an art, irrationally, exultantly, for its own sake." With his "fat, quick hands" and "sad and greedy" eyes, Weiler makes his fortune from the "labors of other men." At the other end of the scale is McDonald's fireman, for whom work is presumably such an urgent economic necessity that he cannot stop to consider its ethical or spiritual merits.

In the middle is McDonald, who builds his railroad "by the power of his strength and love." His respect for the beauty and integrity of his materials preserves in them the spirit of their origins. After lovingly restoring one of his two rusted engines, "so incrusted and immovable that they seemed to be two petrified antediluvians plunged through eternity in their vast bucolic reverie," he builds a fire in the firebox. "Slowly the drivers began to move; with the snort of a bison she turned them over; steam jets hissed beside the ponies; twice more, and she struck her stride. . . ." The energy is clearly spiritual as well as physical, an epic technological manifestation of the epic spiritual energy of man, celebrated earlier by Thoreau and later by Boyd's fellow North Carolinian Thomas Wolfe.

The antithesis in value and in point of view that we see in McDonald and Weiler is a regional one: Weiler is a northerner; McDonald, a southerner. Another of Boyd's stories of the South employs the same antithesis. "Elms and Fair Oaks" is set in the North—at Princeton University (The College of New Jersey) at the time of the Civil War.[19] The story is conventional in plot: two Princeton students, one from Pennsylvania and the other from New Orleans, become intimate friends. The reserved northerner wishes to emulate the gallant ebullience of his southern friend, but he fails to do so until, the war having arrived, he finds himself in command of a Pennsylvania company at Fair Oaks. Coincidentally (Boyd unfortunately found such coincidences attractive all too often), the opposing forces are commanded by his southern friend. In one supreme gesture of gallantry, the Pennsylvanian refrains from giving the command to fire until his friend is out of danger. As in "Old Pines," the point again is that southern values, although produced to an extent by a world that never was, are nevertheless worthy of emulation.

More elaborate than "Elms and Fair Oaks" in contrasting southern and northern attitudes toward life is "Shif'less."[20] Abijah Peabody, a New Englander, arrives in North Carolina with his son Fred to take over a rundown farm. With relentless Yankee industry (which Fred, taking after his southern mother rather than his father, does not share), Peabody transforms the farm into a model of order, cleanliness, and productivity. In the process, he antagonizes his southern neighbors, whom he holds in contempt for their shiftlessness. "Great Land A'mighty," he tells his neighbor Uncle Duncan, "I've done more in the last two months than you have in a year." Duncan is unimpressed. Observing Peabody's obsessive painting of everything in sight, he says, "The old Vaughan place has stood without paint for a hundred years. . . . Heart pine needs no paint; it is full of rosin. You are wasting your time. . . . What have you done? Considerable work—mostly useless. But you have made no friends. . . . Why do you spend your time trying to change the natural order? It does not appear to make you happy." But therein lies the difference. "I wasn't raised to be happy," Peabody replies; "I was raised to work."

Peabody's ire is focused particularly on his son Fred, who prefers to spend his days socializing in the village and his nights coon-hunting with Negroes. In the end, Fred's point of view is vindicated. His apparent shiftlessness is merely a disposition to work with, rather than against, the established order of things— the economic, as well as the social and natural, order.

Three stories that Boyd wrote later in his career—"Blood-hound," "Civic Crisis," and "Away! Away!"—are concerned with the South; but the tone of all of them is humorous rather than serious. In "Bloodhound," written solely in dialogue, a posse of white citizens with a bloodhound pursue a Negro who, they assume, has stolen a suit of clothes. They trail him to Sis High-pockets' house, drag him from beneath the bed, and interrogate Sis about his presence there:

"Sis, what ails you? This is as sorry a nigger as ever I saw. . . ."
"Gentlemens, God is my judge and witness. I never seen this person before. He must have crope under my bed while I was sleeping. . . ."
"Anybody find the suit? Cut open the mattress."
"Done cut it open. . . ."
"Let's get out. Between nigger and feathers I'm about to lose my breath."[21]

"Civic Crisis"[22] deals with the same general subject as "Blood-hound": the tragicomic involvement of Negroes with the law in the white South. On a sidewalk bench outside the police station of a small southern town, Captain MacNutt sits somnolent and undisturbed as crisis after crisis—a fight, a robbery, a house-breaking—is reported to him. With indolent village sages who stroll by, he solemnly discusses the merits of various foxhounds, particularly of Tennessee Sal, the pride of the village. MacNutt is stirred into action only when Eightball, a humorously obse-quious Negro, reports that Tennessee Sal is loose and is being pursued by "Miz Roon's poodle." A real crisis is at hand; the Tennessee Sal blood line is about to be ruined: "Damn you, Eightball, you stay with me. . . . Hey, Proc, grab that poodle. . . . Down the alley. Hey fellows, come on, she's loose, Tennessee Sal. Hotter than—excuse me lady. You, there, cut in the back way, God damn, don't stand there; there she goes! Jesus God, who let that poodle loose? Turn her, turn her . . . catch up that poodle. Can't nobody catch him? Shoot the pink-eyed little son of a bitch. . . ." As in "Bloodhound," judgment of the cynical and self-serving white justice is tempered considerably by the pervasive humor of the story. The narrative point of view is not unlike Fred Peabody's in "Shif'less": man preserves his equa-nimity by sensing the humor in the obvious faults of the system.

In "Away! Away!," the only story Boyd wrote about fox-hunting,[23] MacSherrill, the protagonist, finds himself financially unable to continue the gracious tradition of hunting which his father and grandfather had pursued before him. Plagued by bad luck, circumstance, and debts, he arranges a rigged hunt in order to entice a wealthy northerner to buy an abandoned farm near his own. Although MacSherrill is badly injured in the chase, his ruse works, and he listens in pained delight as his victim tells him that the farm will be bought and that the hunt will become an annual affair. "Give me some more of that stuff," MacSherrill tells the doctor who has come to give him an anesthetic, "I feel so mean." It is a case of folk wisdom and guile getting the best of the naïveté and greed of the northern city slicker—an inversion of the situation in "Old Pines," and the only southern story Boyd wrote that might legitimately be described as a pastoral.

Boyd's most unusual story of the South, "The Gizzard of a Scientist,"[24] is reminiscent of Poe and Hawthorne in subject and tone. Set in a southern coastal town (presumably New Orleans) of the late 1920's, the lazy-warm streets, wisteria-draped doorways, and moss-hung live oaks provide a metaphoric background for the moral laxity of its protagonist, a medical doctor whose addiction to drink is exceeded only by his passion for research. The doctor is an outlander and is fiercely proud of it. "Southern chivalry," he sneers, is "just a high-toned grade of rootiness. . . . [You] sweet-scented cavaliers . . . [are] suckers. Diddling around with your notes and flowers and valentine poems." Women are for men who "haven't anything else," he says. "I've got science."

The doctor has come to the South because "A man needs hospitals and plenty of niggers to work on. Up home everybody would be my friend. I couldn't try anything." Presently, however, he marries a "white-faced girl with soft black hair," beside whom he looks "like a square, cast-iron man." After her accidental death from an incompetently performed tonsillectomy, he realizes he did love and need her. At the end of the story, his closest friend finds him in his laboratory, "slumped stiffly in a chair and whiter than any dead man ever was before. . . . From the bandage around his elbow a thin tube ran to a sheeted figure on the table, to the sharp white angle of a woman's arm. There was a drift of dark hair." Like Aylmer in Hawthorne's "The Birthmark," his sin is unpardonable, and the damage he has wrought is irreparable.

Considered as a group, Boyd's stories of the South possess

considerable unity. Locale is well defined in both time and space; but the setting is decidedly not the vaguely Romantic, "befo' de wah" South; it is not the cotton-culture South at all. It is neither Ellen Glasgow's nor Erskine Caldwell's nor William Faulkner's South; instead, we have the Piedmont South of the 1920's, left in the backwash of history that never even directly touched it. Except for McDonald's, there are no decaying "big houses," no ramshackle tenant houses. The economy of the region is based largely on subsistance agriculture. Its history is a middle history, possessing neither the glorious past of Tidewater Virginia nor the bleak depravity of Georgia tobacco country. And, since the conditions of life in the present are so much like those in the past, we see the quality of life not in images of a once productive but now ruined land, and not in the ruined descendants of once great families, but in the minds of the present generation who are and understand themselves to be at one with their past.

Of the eleven stories Boyd published before 1925, a sense of history is important in five; and four of those five are the more successful ones. Of all twenty stories, the ones involving history in some way are superior to those that do not. Moreover, if we separate the stories that must be called "southern" from those that are predominately "northern," we clearly see that a sense of history as a motif occurs almost inevitably in conjunction with southern settings and protagonists.

It is appropriate that in the last story Boyd published during his lifetime, "Horses in the Sky,"[25] the protagonist is a southern ex-cavalry colonel who as an intelligence officer is observing glider-troop landing maneuvers during World War II and whose sense of history is strong. The colonel sees the glider troops merely as "the newest version" of the "oldest arm" of the army, "the eternal infantry: the sort of men who had formed the Army of Northern Virginia . . . [and] the Army of the Potomac." The difference is minor: they are merely infantry "mounted" on airplanes—"horses in the sky"—instead of the horses on which infantry troops fought as cavalry in the past. The colonel is confident the glider troops will have the same splendid success that the cavalry had, and he is unperturbed by the skepticism of a young officer standing nearby. "It is because you do not know the past," the Colonel says, "that you cannot see the future."

The mind of Boyd's southerners has its beauties as well as its limitations. It is relatively free of the venality and cynicism of the mind of the industrial northerners. Instead of being committed to economic gain, science, and industry, all of which too often require the cynical and inhumane manipulation of people, it is committed to human relationships, which it values above all else. When Uncle Duncan tells Abijah Peabody, "you have made no friends," more is at issue than a point of etiquette. Boyd's people also realize that man must find his place *in* the natural order, rather than try to remake nature according to his own plan. Such a distinction separates Fred Peabody's paradoxically effective "shiftlessness" from his father's meaningless industry. The people of the stories also understand themselves to exist in continuum of time that moves as lazily as the long, hot afternoon; and as a result, they have few driving neuroses. To Peabody's complaint that his indolence has cost him a day's lost working time, the narrator of the story replies, "why, man, I got all the days they is." There is, finally, almost a paradoxical salvation through mediocrity: because the characters' aims are not lofty, the means employed to achieve them are modest; and the inevitable evil and loss that attend the quest are, in most cases, therefore minor.

Boyd's somewhat indulgent admiration for the people he saw around him and used in his stories did not keep him from revealing their obvious faults. We see, for instance, that the southerner's complacency puts him at the mercy of his natural and economic environment, and of his own inertia. He can become the victim of an immobilizing nostalgia or the partisan of active resistance to change. "If things would never change . . ." MacSherrill muses in "Away! Away!" If resistance to change is intense enough, it can make a man immoral, as is pointedly clear in the stories about Negroes. Because the southerner takes himself, his fellows, and his environment so much for granted, he can also profligately waste his substance. The scrub oaks that replace the mighty pines on McDonald's ancestral acres represent a tragedy of the first order.

Boyd's reputation does not and should not rest upon his short stories, even though bits of his best work may be found in them. He himself regarded many of them as apprentice pieces; with a very few exceptions, they should be so regarded. The flaws in them are too numerous and too obvious to be overlooked.

For instance, that most ancient and most fundamental fact of southern life—the Negro-white dichotomy—is treated in the stories in a manner that does not bear intense scrutiny. White people are guilty of a radically unjust, shabbily condescending paternalism that degrades both themselves and Negroes, but they are rarely judged for it. We are compelled to sense the grotesque humor of the situation, but we are not really allowed, at the same time, to see its tragedy. Negroes in the stories are always patronized, and most of them are stereotypes. There is no truly admirable Negro in the stories—no Dilsey who endures, no Lucas Beauchamp. The greatest single failure of the southern stories is not that they fail to portray Negroes as the suffering servants of southern society but that they give no Negro his own identity, however far beneath white middle-class standards one may feel compelled to make it, given the unfortunate facts of the Negro's actual situation.[26]

We cannot, however, afford to disregard the stories entirely. In subject, theme, tone, and style they are an index to Boyd's later work in the novel; taken together, they form a substantial body of writing.

CHAPTER 3

Two Novels of War:
Drums and *Marching On*

I   Drums *(1925)*

S HORTLY after Boyd began *Drums*, his first novel, he observed that "Literature in [America], while showing many
hopeful symptoms ... [is] divided between the old virtue-
triumphant school of false sentiment and false heroic and the
new writers who, while much more skillful technically and truer
to the superficial aspects of life, are oriental in their basic ...
regard [for] man as a helpless puppet in the clutch of circumstances or of his own passions. [But] ... all of English literature
has been devoted to the idea of man beset with trials and
temptations and sometimes overwhelmed by them but frequently
victorious and if not the master of his fate at least capable of
modifying and alleviating it."[1]

The observation provides an insight into Boyd's intentions
for the five novels he wrote. It also defines the point at which
both the novels themselves and their importance in the history
of American fiction have been misunderstood. During his career,
Boyd was known as a Realist who was doing something new
in the historical novel. Since his death, however, he has more
often been dismissed as a writer of historical romances not
unlike those of Sir Walter Scott and his imitators.[2] Actually,
there is some truth in both assessments, for Boyd's novels are
transitional in two senses. He had successfully used the techniques of psychological Realism before he even began his first
novel, but throughout his career he remained to an extent bound
by certain Romantic conventions. On the other hand, he
questioned any of the materialistic assumptions of Realism that
tended to strip man of his dignity.

As Ernest Leisy has suggested, *Drums* is pivotal in the revitalization of the American historical novel. But the "new" historical
novel may itself be more important than has been realized in
broadening the scope of contemporary fiction in general. Earlier
historical fiction now seems barren because it is not faithful to
the realities of man's divided nature; Realistic fiction is apt to
seem sterile when it does not admit that man has a history in
which he has shown moments of greatness as well as depravity,
and in the course of which in any event he has become what he
presently is.

My thesis is that *Drums* does not employ Romantic conventions to a sufficient degree to allow one to call it a historical
romance; that the degree of psychological Realism is far greater
than that we find in earlier historical novels, but is not linked to
philosophical determinism in point of view; and that the use of
history in *Drums* surpasses that of earlier historical novels in
sophistication and helps point the way toward the inculcation
of a historical dimension in the modern psychological novel.

II *Finding a Subject*

The history of American Realism is, in one sense, character-
ized by the discovery of literary materials in the common fabric
of American life—dialect, frontier humor, local color, and more
recently, myth. Not surprisingly, the discovery has often been
realized within fairly narrow regional boundaries—by Joel
Chandler Harris in Georgia, George Washington Cable in New
Orleans, and Ellen Glasgow in Virginia, for instance. In the
early 1920's, North Carolina had no writers. Although it had had
a few of minor stature, it could claim no William Gilmore Simms,
Henry Timrod, Sidney Lanier, Harris, or Cable. In 1921, its
literary resources were virtually untapped. Thomas Wolfe was
still in George Pierce Baker's 47 Workshop at Harvard,
Paul Green was studying philosophy at Cornell, and Frederick
Koch's Carolina Playmakers were still in their infancy. As
Jonathan Daniels later observed, James Boyd began to give
North Carolina a literature "before it had native writers of
its own."[3]

North Carolina, Boyd said, was "the least romantic but most
distinctive and solid of the southern states," and the North
Carolinian was "a man in whom hardy . . . independence has

been tempered by a touch of Southern courtesy, a man ignorant and narrow but astute ... slipshod but self-reliant and resourceful, intolerant but high-principled, hospitable but with few real loyalties outside his own family, slow to argue but a tremendous fighter."[4] As the subject for his first novel, Boyd chose the American Revolution in North Carolina. Neither alienated nor expatriated as so many of his contemporaries were after World War I, he found in the still vital history of North Carolina and the South that tie which Malcolm Cowley says that he and his friends lacked—the tie to the past which provided perspective for their present experience.

Boyd began writing *Drums* late in 1921 or early in 1922, partially at the suggestion of John Galsworthy, who had visited briefly in Moore County and had read some of his stories.[5] Although hindered by the "lack of recorded local history," Boyd finished the book by early 1924 and signed a contract with Maxwell Perkins of Scribner's.[6]

Drums, which went on sale March 27, 1925, and was successful with both the critics and the public, is concerned simultaneously with the forging of a national identity and with the development of a young man's consciousness. Johnny Fraser, son of Loyalist Scotch Presbyterian John Fraser, emigrant veteran of the Battle of Culloden (1745), and prosperous farmer in the Little River section of piedmont North Carolina, comes of age during the decade preceding the revolution and is sent to the port city of Edenton to be educated as a gentleman by the clergyman Dr. Clapton, also a loyalist.

In Edenton, Johnny meets Captain Flood, an uncouth riverboat captain; Sir Nathaniel Dukinfield; His Majesty's Collector of the Port, Captain Tennant and his daughter Eve; and sundry planters of the colony—all of whom eventually provide him with a broader education than his father had intended. As news of war drifts in from other colonies and violence breaks out in Edenton, Johnny returns home, shaken by the spectacle of the immaculate Captain Tennant being forced to quit Edenton amid the raucous and abusive taunts of the townspeople. A few months later, newly disenchanted with his crude country neighbors, Johnny embarks for England to secure his father's savings against the coming revolution. He spends two years as a junior clerk in a London counting house, passing his leisure hours with the now repatriated Eve Tennant. While on a trip to Scotland for a friend in North Carolina, he is induced to join the crew of the then unknown Captain John Paul Jones, whom he had previously met in Edenton. Wounded in a subsequent battle, Johnny returns to North Carolina. A year later he fights with a North Carolina brigade that helps defeat Tarleton's Dragoons.

Even so brief a summary shows that numerous conventions of the historical romance are present in *Drums*. The protagonist is infatuated with a young maiden (Eve Tennant) who is above his station but not above his moral deserts; he becomes intimate with important historical personages; he proves his physical and moral courage against persons of superior strength and training; and he fights with uncommon valor in an epic battle (the *Bonhomme Richard* versus the *Serapis.*) We may judge the concessions to convention less severely if we are aware of certain facts of history (the planter Wylie Jones and his friend Joseph Hewes *did* frequent Hornblower's Tavern in Edenton, and Joseph Hewes *did* secure John Paul Jones his commission in the Continental navy); but the conventions are there, nevertheless.

Unfortunately, the conventions have been allowed to overshadow the merits of the novel that early reviewers recognized. E. C. Beckwith of the New York *Evening Post* declared that *Drums,* being free of the "standardized puerilities" normally associated with its subject, was "the finest novel of the American Revolution that has yet been written."[7] H. L. Pangborn said Boyd had "much growing to do before he can aspire to the stature of a Thackeray, but [*Drums*] indicates that he belongs to that family rather than among the writers of romance...."[8] And, in regard to the issue of romance in the novel, another reviewer said Boyd "will someday be ... one of our best," but at present *lacks* "that curious quality of romance" that distinguishes his contemporaries.[9]

In a review in the Harrisburg *Patriot,* Laurence Stallings suggested a useful comparison between *Drums* and Winston Churchill's *Richard Carvel* (1899) which, at the time was the most recent novel about the revolution.[10] By pursuing the comparison, which Stallings resolved strongly in favor of *Drums,* we may demonstrate how relatively free *Drums* is of Romantic convention and how far it surpasses its predecessors both in historical authenticity and in psychological Realism.

As a historical novel, *Richard Carvel* is by the standards of
its own time conventional (and by those of the present, primitive) in form, point of view, use of historical materials, and
psychological analysis. The order of narration is strictly sequen-
tial. The numerous subplots involve stock heroes and villains
whose love affairs, duels, and intrigues occur with tiresome
frequency. The first-person point of view, although obscured
by an antique narrative device (These "memoirs of my grandfather" were not meant to be published, the narrator tells us[11]),
is nostalgic, sentimental, and moralistic. "No psychology, no
sociology or economics, no philosophy, no realism, idealism or
pragmatism troubled my soul . . . when I wrote it," says Churchill in the Preface (1914). "Patriotism was—patriotism. . . . Villains
were villains. . . . Religion was religion. . . . The course of true
love . . . [culminated inevitably in] marital bliss." Unfortunately,
such sentimentality extends into the texture of the novel. "Mr.
Carvel's townhouse in Annapolis stands today . . . a mournful
relic of a glory that is past," the narrator laments. When even
the thin veil of historical perspective is absent, the sentimentality
becomes maudlin. "How those Christmas times of my childhood
come sweeping back on my memory!" Carvel says. And, when
absent for a time from his beloved, he sighs, "Her locket I wore
over my heart. It had lain upon hers."

Churchill's use of historical materials is scarcely more successful. His assessment of the revolutionary era is simplistic ("King
George the Third is alone to blame . . ." for the war, Carvel
concludes), and he takes a cavalier attitude toward the inherent
demand of the historical novel for continuity ("This is not a
history, my dears, . . . and time is growing short. I shall pass
over that dreary summer of '74."). But these faults, serious as
they are, are less significant than Churchill's failure to integrate
historical events with the fortunes of the protagonist.

A principal value of the historical novel, after all, is that it
allows the microcosmic fortunes of one man and the macro-
cosmic movements of history to mirror and illuminate each other
mutually—to serve as reciprocal metaphors by virtue of which
the smaller drama provides emotional focus for the larger, and
the larger provides historical scale and philosophical depth for
the smaller. In *Richard Carvel*, such integration is minimal; the
story of Richard Carvel and the events preceding the revolution
touch each other only tangentially. Carvel helps to rescue a

merchant suspected of violating the colony's embargo on tea, for instance, but he is more eager to avoid a public breach of decorum than to prevent a violation of political principle. In general, he is little interested in defining his political allegiances. It is his position that is threatened by the revolution, not his identity. The reverse is true for Johnny Fraser.

The failure of *Richard Carvel* does not derive wholly from Churchill's portrayal of a single character, however. He fails to provide any character with complex psychological motives, and he therefore deprives them all of significant encounter with complex historical issues. Moved as they are by unrelieved malice, pure virtue, chivalric honor, and the like, they cannot sense the correspondence between individual choice and public policy, or between personal and national identity, since in each case the latter is predicated on compromise. Even when the occasion virtually demands an explanation of what are undoubtedly complex motives, none is forthcoming; at the crucial juncture when John Paul Jones chooses loyalty to America instead of to his hard-won position in London society, Carvel observes, "It is often difficult to lay finger upon the causes which change the drift of a man's opinions, and so I never wholly knew why John Paul abandoned his deep-rooted purpose."

Drums is in some aspects similar to *Richard Carvel*, but is sharply distinguished from it in its achievement of both psychological and historical Realism. The former can be seen in Johnny Fraser's role as protagonist in the apprenticeship novel that is one half of *Drums*, and the latter in the related political and social revolution that composes the other half. Since Johnny's ambivalent response to the revolution is central in the novel, there is an implicit rejection not only of Romantic attitudes toward the past or to a particular historic epoch but also of simplistic conceptions of human personality and human value as a basis for prose fiction.

Johnny's education occurs in three stages: under his father's eye at Little River; under the mutually contradictory instruction of Clapton, Sir Nat, and Wylie Jones in Edenton; and under the condescending guidance of the Tennants in London. John Fraser, who insists that his son shall become "a gentleman in learning as he is in birth," does not realize that such an aim is at variance with his own Protestant ethic. He has no use for "dirty, lawless, and drunken" democrats who respect neither "the word of God [nor] the law of their King, let alone . . . the gentry and the better classes."[12] But, in Edenton, Johnny has trouble remaining faithful to the role his father projects, so attractive are the alternatives.

Johnny's official tutor, Dr. Clapton, tries to teach him his Latin; but meanwhile, he is preoccupied with his own scholarship, which amounts after years of diligence to "a number of sheets of manuscript, written with exquisite care and then crossed neatly out" (97). But Johnny finds Captain Flood more attractive than his tutor. Clapton is paralyzed by his awareness of the infinite possibilities for speculation upon experience; Captain Flood moves freely in a comfortably defined system, and there is a primitive logic in what he says: "At sea, boy, there's a rule for everything and the less a man thinks and the more rules he knows the better off he is"(61).

Johnny is even more attracted to Sir Nat, a charming, world-weary, and somewhat dissipated baronet he meets in Edenton. Sir Nat's judgments of men are as concrete as Clapton's are abstract, and they are every whit as practical as Flood's. "Powerful minds—powerful," he says of two patriot leaders. "But . . . don't know life. No blood horses. No game-birds. Can't shoot. Can't ride. Can't drink. Too bad"(77). From Sir Nat, Johnny learns the subtleties of cock-fighting, gambling, and horse racing; and he finds, to his confusion, that they are all more interesting than Latin.

Captain Tennant and his daughter are intolerably snobbish aristocrats. Johnny is intimidated by the mysterious social usages of their household, and especially by Tennant's harsh judgment of Americans, most of whom he considers "a low-bred pack of scoundrels" (148). Although Johnny eventually becomes recognized as "a young man of quality" (156), the multiplicity of tutors and the variety of available and attractive roles leave him confused and frustrated after nearly two years in Edenton. He welcomes the opportunity to return home: "A raw October wind wheeled leaden clouds heavily across the sky. . . . Dead leaves drifted down the street. . . . Life in him was suspended. . . . [One] thing remained, to creep home, home to the sheltering forest . . ." (151).

His education has affected him more than he realizes, however; he finds life intolerable in Little River, where people "not only [lack] all grace themselves, but . . . [suspect] it in others"

(183). In contrast, London seems to promise grace and excitement; but Johnny is again disillusioned. With Captain Tennant at the exclusive Brooks Club, he watches men at the gaming tables in "rigidly controlled intensity, devoted to an end . . . so far removed from life . . . " (356). The mask itself is hideous enough, but when he sees behind it, his disillusionment is complete. When a vagabond, obviously near death, stumbles into the club, the men, instead of helping him, wager on whether he will die before a doctor arrives (364). Having come to know society at all levels, Johnny sees that its values are "not authoritative" (345). Both ends of the social-political spectrum have been discredited; neither of the settled, defined alternatives Johnny has been so much at pains to choose between remains as an acceptable option. Freedom from allegiance to either makes absolute the anxiety that previously was limited.

As Johnny tries to define a new role for himself, we see how much more complex a creation he is than his counterpart in *Richard Carvel*. From childhood, he has yearned idealistically for adventure. Staring into the fire in his father's house at Little River, he saw "swords and shields and drifting smoke. . . . [A] charred log burst in flame . . . [and] took form. Black towers raised their heads, from the battlements flames waved like banners . . ." (6f.). The idealism is manifest in more mature ways as Johnny grows older, but it remains essentially intact—and it clashes repeatedly with the actual quality of his experience. When the colonists begin to resist the tyranny of George III, the result is not an enhancement of human dignity but a debasement not only of values but of the quality of life in society. Nor is the disillusionment confined to the colonies, as the Brooks Club episode eventually makes clear.

Over and over, Johnny's ideal expectations turn out to be sinister illusions (57) until he finds himself at length in France, where he meets Sir Nat again. Sir Nat's subsequent death in a tavern fight in which he and Johnny attempt to defend the patriot cause, leads Johnny to ponder the ultimate bases for belief and action in the world. Musing at Sir Nat's grave, he concludes that it is "incredible that a man so simple, so kindly . . . could die. Historical figures . . . died, of course. . . . [But for a man] who wished to accomplish nothing, to influence no one . . . death seemed grotesquely out of scale" (422f.). Sir Nat's death raises fundamental questions: Is there a moral order in the universe? Can it, if it exists, be realized in society and politics? What is the balance of nobility and depravity in human nature? Johnny does not consider all of the questions immediately, but after Nat's death he is never able to escape them. His own acts, whatever they are to be, must now be seen in a larger context.

In deciding finally to join the patriot cause, Johnny does not reject his idealism; he simply recognizes the fundamental paradox of politics and human institutions: institutions set up to serve ideals do not, because of their inherent imperfections, deny the validity of the ideals. "Here lay one who had lived according to his simple creed and when the moment came, had struck his blow," he observes of Sir Nat. The universe is neither perfectly moral nor perfectly rational, but it does allow limited action in the service of viable ideals.

This paradox is only one of many that occur both in the personal drama of Johnny Fraser and in the larger drama of the revolution. The two dramas are metaphors for each other. Johnny Fraser's explicit conflict is between two ways of life, and it involves essentially a question of identity. But the implied question is that of political commitment, seen explicitly in the war. On the other hand, the explicit conflict in the war is over political alignment; but, implicitly, the issue is that of identity in terms of either a democratic or an aristocratic assessment of human nature, which is seen explicitly in Johnny's conflict.

The device is similar but not identical to the plot and over-plot method of Elizabethan drama, in which essentially the same action occurs on two different levels at the same time. In *Drums*, however, there are not two "levels," one of which can be called more general or important than the other. *Drums* is neither more nor less Johnny Fraser's story than it is the story of the revolution. (In this respect it is strikingly distinct from *Richard Carvel.*) Neither is less fully defined than the other; if either is chosen as foreground or vehicle of the metaphor, as it may be because of the inherent balance of the narrative, the other becomes background or tenor.[13]

For the metaphors to be valid reciprocally, the subtlety of Johnny's psychological motivation, which we have already seen, must be matched by a subtle handling of the revolution as a historical phenomenon. This raises the whole issue of historical detail and authenticity in the novel: How accurately is the era recreated? How sophisticated is the novel's view of history? How intimate is the relationship between the actions of characters and the issues of history?

"All that I had . . . I put into it," Churchill says in the Preface to *Richard Carvel*. "I lived, as I composed it, in old Annapolis and in old London. Charles James Fox and John Paul Jones were my companions, and I tried faithfully to interpret their characters, to depict the environment and customs of their times."[14] The author of a historical novel may learn about the past through scholarly research, but the past becomes valid for his reader only when the author is able to give it an existence in the novel that is wholly independent of his own personality. In effect, the reader is being asked to trust the "history" in the novel *because* he trusts the author's assertions about his own relationship to the facts he has discovered. Boyd's prefatory note to *Drums* is different from Churchill's in content as well as in tone: "In this book the main facts of history have been followed except in two cases: the *Bonhomme Richard* did not sail from Brest but from Lorient; the incident of the vagabond in Chapter XXXV did not occur at Brooks's Club but at another club in London." The voice is passive; the author's personality does not enter even implicitly in the narrative point of view. Consequently, in the narrative itself, the "and now, my dears" authorial intrusions that we find in *Richard Carvel* are wholly absent.

Boyd visited sites where major scenes of *Drums* were to be laid, but the bulk of his research was in scholarly sources.[15] Important primary sources included the *Colonial Records of North Carolina 1662-1776*, the *State Records of North Carolina 1777-1790*, the published orderly books of the Continental army, and J. S. Barnes's *Logs of Serapis-Alliance-Ariel Under Jones' Command* (1911). These works were supplemented by the few available newspapers, such as the Cape Fear *Mercury;* the diaries and memoirs of William Byrd, William Moultrie, Ethan Allen, and others; the biographies and published letters of such figures as the North Carolina Federalist leader James Iredell; and the journals of foreign travelers in North Carolina.

Secondary sources included general histories of the Revolution such as George Trevelyan's four-volume *American Revolution* (1909-12); state and local histories such as John Spencer Bassett's account of the North Carolina Regulators and William

K. Boyd's *History of North Carolina 1783-1860* (1919); works on special topics such as Alfred T. Mahan's *The Influence of Sea Power upon History, 1660-1783*; and books by W. E. B. Du Bois and Ulrich B. Phillips on slavery and the slave trade. Secondary sources also included imaginative literature, both English and American, related to the period: the Restoration dramatists and the novelists Smollett, Sterne, Thackeray, and others. References in Boyd's research file to American literature include the obvious works, such as the novels of Churchill; the works of Harold Frederic, John Pendleton Kennedy, Edward Eggleston, and Walt Whitman; and the little-known early nineteenth-century Virginia novelist William Alexander Carruthers.

Boyd's use of his sources was quite varied. On the card for Thackeray's *The Virginians*, for example, he noted, "useful only as picture of Stuart England in London & Wells at beginning of Revolution." But among the hundreds of cards about the written and spoken language of the period, many are drawn from *The Virginians*, even though it was not the kind of novel Boyd had intended to write. He was apparently interested not in literary models but in a sense of the authentic texture of life in the eighteenth century. More than a thousand other cards on such topics as commerce, military operations, education, folkways, orthography, transportation, domestic architecture, and government suggest the effort he expended to gain that sense. The cards on language, for instance, are divided into subcategories according to occupations and social classes, and those subcategories are divided into parts of speech.

We are not surprised that the dialogue in *Drums* rings completely true, or, more largely, that we finish the novel with the sense that it is true to more than the "main facts" of history. Boyd's prefatory note is actually an understatement. In *Richard Carvel*, characters dress, act, and speak in a vaguely eighteenth-century way; but specific historical detail, when it occurs, is generally of the stereotyped wig and waistcoat variety. Characters who should differ greatly from each other are almost indistinguishable in dress and speech. For the celebrated figures of the Revolution, Churchill accepts the Parson Weems stereotypes. "His very person seemed to exhale, not sanctity, but virility," Carvel says of George Washington. "In his presence self-command came to me, as a virtue gone out of him."[16]

In *Drums*, we find not only the expected large details of major political, social, and military events but also minute details that allow the general historical authenticity to penetrate into the very fabric of the novel: the frayed-twig toothbrushes hanging beside the well curb; the "varnished chintz hat-box" under Johnny's bed in Edenton; and Wylie Jones's glass coach, "its lacquered saffron panels well streaked with forty miles of country clay." The wonder is that such detail never becomes oppressive. At its best, the effect is poetic: lying in bed in his father's house at Little River, Johnny notes that the roof "still held the dregs of night where, here and there, the tip of a shingle-peg caught the light and twinkled like a morning star" (10).[17]

With one lamentable exception (the stereotyped Negroes), the characters in *Drums* act and speak not only as representatives of distinctly identifiable classes and conditions of life but also as unique individuals within that class or condition. Sir Nat and Captain Tennant are both English aristocrats but are very different from each other; Battle, Hewes, and Jones are all American aristocrats, but again they differ from each other, as well as from their English counterparts; and Captain Flood and Cassoway G. Jenny, the South Carolina pack-horse man, are distinct representatives of the self-parodying lower class of white people who pretend to position and elegance.

It is not finally the greater historiographical sophistication or the more pervasive, authentic, and deftly handled historical detail that places *Drums* so far beyond *Richard Carvel* as a historical novel; it is the fact that views of history, rather than history itself, become the substance of the novel. Events in *Richard Carvel* have neither actual consequences nor philosophical implications that extend very far outside the immediate situations involving the characters themselves. But, for many of the characters in *Drums,* the problem of action is inseparable from the necessity for self-identification, which in turn is bound up with the question of the nature and meaning of history. Dr. Clapton's attitude toward The Work, "The Sminthiad, or the Cosmopolis of Smiths," is a case in point. The plan of The Work "presents peculiar difficulties," he tells Johnny. "In most works of the kind... it is customary to begin with earliest times and lead down to the present.... [But it] should be obvious that the age which is most familiar to us is the age in which we live. The present, then, forms the point of departure, from which

I lead the reader further and further into the past. The difficulty is, however, that with each addition to my knowledge ... of recent times, a new introduction must be written"(99). We may smile at Clapton's impracticality, but his problem is serious —to achieve historical perspective amid the flux of history.

For all of the characters except Clapton, the questions of history present themselves in somewhat narrower terms—the nature and significance of the revolution. (We note that in *Richard Carvel* this issue is usually resolved in terms of simple self-interest. "After a deal of thought on the subject," Carvel says, "I decided for a while at least, to show no political leanings at all"). To Johnny's father, the coming revolution is no holy war; it is another manipulation of the common people by the aristocrats for their own purposes, in which "the rich will surrender their luxuries and the poor their necessities"(20).

Minor characters also confront the issue. The Fraser's neighbor James Merrillee lives in a dream world of Classical history, from which he views the Revolution as he naïvely assumes it would have been seen by an Athenian orator. "If a spark of the primal virtue with which our first forebears in their perfect state of nature were endowed survives in us," he tells Johnny, "we shall rise, strike off the fetters, reclaim our long lost heritage, form a new state where every law is just, every man free!"(274). Meanwhile, Merrillee's farm goes to ruin, and he himself is later needlessly killed in the war when he tries single-handedly to storm a stone house full of British soldiers. He "hollered out some Latin motto and he ran for the house," his wife says bitterly. "He was a fool!" (484). And Cassoway Jenney's description of his "ancestral domain" in South Carolina parodies not only his own pretension but also the view of history that has given rise to such pretensions among the emerging southern agragian aristocracy: "It is impossible, ma'm," he tells Mrs. Fraser,

to depict the brilliance of the scene in those days, now, alas, no more, when the first families of the Province, the Governor and numerous distinguished visitors from England—where the famous Castle Jenney still attests the distinction of our family's parent stock—were lavishly entertained regardless of *ex*pense. It was hyer, in the Temple of Venus on the South Lawn, that Major Munkittrick of the Charleston Independent Company declared himself to Miss Susie Pellew; the grotto was the haunt of the learned Doctor Wolp of Wolp's Neck ... and the sunken walk was the scene of the duel between Colonel Popple and Gen. Brashay which terminated so happily fo' all concerned. (43)

The point of view presented here for comic and satiric effect is close to that held seriously by Richard Carvel.

Not every instance of an inadequate understanding of history leads to tragedy, but every one is eventually condemned either by the pattern of action in the novel or by satirical humor. Cassoway G. Jenney is one case in point; another is the rooms in Wiley Jones's house which are named "Parnassus," "Olympus," "Delphi," "Illium," and the like, revealing the pretentious and bogus analogy between Greek civilization and southern aristocracy (or more largely, of course, the American experiment itself).

If one view of history in the novel is finally viable, it is Johnny's. Contemplating the death of Sir Nat, he sees that, since the movements of history can destroy the little dignity possible in man's experience, Sir Nat's personality can have its final validity only in an ideal, transhistorical sense. But Sir Nat *acted* in history, and his action suggests that—although the universe may not make sense morally, and the war may not make complete sense politically, socially, or esthetically—a man must nevertheless "strike his blow" in defense of his values. By so doing, he shows himself, "if not master of his fate at least capable of modifying and alleviating it," and of defining the context in which it has meaning.

If it is true that the historical novel has been enriched by the use of Realistic techniques, it is also true that the reinvigorated historical novel has contributed something to the modern Realistic psychological novel. Questions concerning the nature and operation of history, and of human response to it, are now very much a part of the materials available to the novelist. It is no accident that Jack Burden, the narrator of Robert Penn Warren's *All the King's Men,* is an erstwhile doctoral candidate in history; nor is it fortuitous that Robert Jordan regrets, as he dies heroically at the end of Hemingway's *For Whom the Bell Tolls,* that his grandfather who fought in the Civil War is not there to see him. To insist that such emphasis has come wholly because of developments in the historical novel would be indefensible, but to deny the importance of the connection would be equally ridiculous.

Drums ends with Johnny Fraser watching a column of North
Carolina militia march past his house. In the description we
feel intensely the thread of historical continuity that links them
to each other and to the earth as they move through both space
and time: "[These] Militia seemed to feel the need of rhythm.
Perhaps they hoped that its compelling bond . . . would help,
at least, to weld them into one. Perhaps . . . they had learned
that only rhythm could carry them through endless months of
marching so far beyond their powers. Even now they seemed
to draw their strength . . . from its profound, sombre intoxica-
tion. . . . The earth was trembling to their inexorable monotone"
(489). The vignette is not only a comment on the relation of
human acts to the processes of history, but the metaphor also
for Boyd's next novel, *Marching On.*

III   Marching On (1927)

By November, 1924, months before *Drums* went on sale, Boyd
was well into his second novel; in September, 1926, he sent the
manuscript to Maxwell Perkins.[18] *Marching On* was published
in the spring of 1927 and was a popular success almost immediately, but the critics were less enthusiastic than they had been
for *Drums.* Some reviewers noted that something new had
been done with the Civil War as a subject, but only Morris
Markey went so far as to say Boyd "has done for the Southern
soldier what Stephen Crane did for the Northern soldier, and
. . . has done it somewhat better."[19] The most important review
was by James Southall Wilson, who found *Marching On* inferior
to *Drums;* but he pointed out that, like *Drums,* it contributed
to the transformation of the historical novel as a form and would
therefore be read by many people "who would today find the
historical novel of twenty years ago . . . pretentiously dull." Both
novels, Wilson said, gave "new significance to an old story."[20]

Marching On is an "old story" in two senses: it is to a degree
a rewriting of *Drums* (as Wilson observed), and it employs a
few elements common to Civil War fiction long before 1927.
Parallels between Boyd's first two novels are abundant; some
of the same characters, more or less transformed, appear in both;
the dichotomy between aristocratic and democratic ideas and
sensibilities is marked; the point of view is a middle-class one
in both cases; and the protagonist comes to maturity in the war.

But there is a change in scale in treating the war, a change in tone, in the balance between the fortunes of the protagonist and the large movements of history, and in metaphor and theme.

The story of *Marching On* is simple and in some ways conventional. James Fraser, son of a poor-white North Carolina farmer, becomes infatuated with Stewart Prevost, daughter of a nearby planter.[21] After several futile attempts to call on her, he goes east to work in the shops of the Wilmington and Weldon Railroad. His experiences in the streets and taverns of the Wilmington waterfront district reinforce his prejudices against Negroes, sons of planters, and northerners, particularly of the Abolitionist variety. Fraser falters briefly after talking with a schoolteacher who has read Helper's *The Impending Crisis* (1857); but, when Fort Sumter falls, Fraser returns home to join a company of Confederate infantry financed by Colonel Prevost and commanded by his son Charles.

James renews his courtship of Stewart Prevost, again without success, but this time not without hope. After his company joins the Army of Northern Virginia, he fights in Stonewall Jackson's Shenandoah Valley campaign and is taken prisoner. Many months later he is exchanged and sent home. When Fort Fisher falls, the last hope of the Confederacy in North Carolina disappears; but the destruction of the Prevost plantation and of the system that supported it frees Stewart to marry James Fraser.

Although the marriage is in the tradition of the historical romance, *Marching On* is actually freer of romantic convention than *Drums*. James Fraser is never called upon to defend his personal honor; he fights neither more nor less bravely than we might expect in battles that are neither more nor less important than hundreds of others (compare Johnny and the *Bonhomme Richard*); and the few "great men" (such as Stonewall Jackson) who appear are seen from a proper distance.

In *Marching On* Boyd sought to avoid not only most of the literary conventions associated with his subject but the point of view as well. The "flowered romances of cavaliers, old rosewood, [and] faithful servitors" were "merely a fraction of the truth," he said, a "fraction small beyond belief. . . . [The] shining plantations of our dreams were the merest, the tiniest oases in a lifeless desert of the human spirit, a mournful, dreary land through which a man could travel days on end, seeing only men and women sunk in lethargy, clothed like savages, housed like swine."[22] *Marching On,* he said, was "about a state of society that had reduced many white men as well as most negroes to serfdom and about how the war, putting a strain on this unsound structure, broke it down, freeing black and white alike."[23]

But, if Boyd held this essentially revisionist view of the war, why is the novel marred by an extremely improbable and furtive romance between a lowborn young man and the impossibly beautiful daughter of an impossibly genteel planter? Why must James Fraser pursue Stewart Prevost with an ardor no less distinguished for its purity than for its pertinacity, until at last the two are united? We might assume that Boyd shared Churchill's conviction that there *was* a time when "The course of true love, after much turning and twisting and tumbling, fell [inevitably] into the lake of marital bliss."[24]

Maxwell Perkins repeatedly expressed doubts about the love story, and it is futile to argue that it is not a blemish, as Boyd himself eventually saw. "[It] is the greatest, or certainly the most vital, mistake that I have ever made and I never cease to regret it," he later told Bernard DeVoto. "Assuming that all three [characters] were typical, as they were meant to be, James Fraser could not have been accepted by the Colonel and his daughter."[25] The romance is not, however, quite the defect that Boyd's comment implies; it is by no means *merely* a sentimental overlay of "romantic interest," a concession to the conventions of historical romance.

While the Fraser-Prevost romance does not cease to be, in one sense, a defect in the esthetic design of the novel, nor in itself an imperfect thing, it is organically related to the central theme: that the Civil War forced the South to become democratic,[26] and replaced a widely diffused romantic cast of mind with a more realistic one. Although Boyd felt that "a too single-hearted devotion to a philosophical ideal led me to the same mistake as that consistently committed by the most meretricious of romances,"[27] careful attention to the nature and implications of that ideal reveals that *Marching On* differs radically from the "meretricious romances" in that the Romantic version of the lower-class partisans of the Confederate cause never escapes the judgment demanded by the Realistic texture of the novel. By presenting that vision, *Marching On* achieves part of its historical authenticity and psychological validity; by judging it, it judges an inherently pernicious view of history. As Henry Seidel Canby says in his Introduction to Stephen Vincent Benét's *John Brown's Body*, the Civil War is "almost necessarily seen by a realistic age . . . in terms of realism as well as romance."[28] To ignore either view would be to present an incomplete picture of the era.

Marching On begins by considering the spiritual consequences of the feudal southern economic system. James Fraser sees that his hard-working father does not prosper "according to his deserts." Rice planters like Prevost have the best land, his father says, "and anyhow it takes niggers to make rice."[29] Moreover, economic inequities are reinforced by the paradoxically dual role of nature itself, which is Prevost's partner, but Fraser's adversary: "[Only] the cotton patch and the wisp of smoke relieved the vast and mournful scene; all else was dark pine forest and darker cypress swamp . . . a shadowy underworld . . . unreal and lifeless" (3). Nature lulls the poor whites with "a sense that things were as they were, immemorial, unchanged, and unchangeable" (69). But to yield to the "drowsy security" of the "hot, dead, humid air" is to sleep the sleep of death. The Frasers rise every morning "to fight their tireless enemies, the crab-grass and the flies"; but after months "stumbling through burning sand" behind the plow, James manages to clear only "a little breathless pocket in the forest" (35). And as surely as it frustrates Fraser's efforts to carve out a space for himself in the "primeval world" (13), nature collaborates with the rice planters whose prosperity depends on the long, hot, humid summers.

Fraser's fight against nature is, in another sense, a fight to preserve his separateness from the "crackers" and the animals they so closely resemble. Nature and the socioeconomic structure prohibit all attempts to rise, but falling is an imminent possibility. In a moment of unguarded wrath, James's face resembles that of "a puzzled, angry dog" (8). "I wish to God I'd busted that yellow rice-hand with my maul," he rages, slipping into the animallike behavior associated with the depraved crackers, of whom the "rat-faced" Racker twins and the demented Sal Scroggs are the most pathetic examples.

Paradoxically, although class consciousness is strong at every level, there are only two classes—the planters, and another class that includes poor whites, "crackers," and Negroes. There

is little substantial difference between the quality of life of the
poor whites and that of the "crackers," as they both seem to
realize when they meet democratically around the shabby grave
of Sal Scroggs. Colonel Prevost's courtesy prompts him to attend the funeral, but both he and they recognize that he can
join their communion only in some eschatological realm.
"Friends," intones Mr. Roon at the graveside, "what do we see
and behold on this mo'nful day? We see not only the lowly, but
the high and mighty gathered together. . . . And so it will be
on the day of jedgement" (31).

It is also a paradox that the largely specious distinctions between the lower classes are a major motivation for members of
those classes. What does not exist in fact is maintained by
appearance. On his way to seek work from Colonel Prevost,
James fingers the black square tie his mother has instructed
him to put on before he reaches the gate at Beaumont, lest
"the Colonel's niggers . . . take him for a cracker" (9). James
Fraser's fight against nature and his struggle toward the world
of Stewart Prevost become then *one* struggle against the tendency to dehumanization inherent in both the natural order
and in the socioeconomic system.

Fraser has essentially the same problem as his remote name-
sake in *Drums*: his inner world is romantic, but his expectations
are consistently frustrated by reality. On an errand to the
plantation to deliver a load of fence rails, Fraser glimpses
Stewart Prevost and feels his spirit "[steal] away, on and upward, leaving his body far behind." Stewart's commonplace
"You have brought a lot of rails" leaves him incredulous "that
she should not have noticed the . . . vast enchantments through
which . . . [he] had passed" (71).

The problem is larger than Stewart's matter-of-fact response,
however. James has sought her because his emotional and
esthetic needs cannot be satisfied in his own world. He plays
the fiddle expertly, but the energy demanded by and released
through his playing is repressed rather than freed by the world
he really belongs in: "By touching the strings with all the soft-
ness in the world, he could just sketch in a tune or two without awakening the others. That was important—not to disturb
the others . . . and not to be disturbed" (62). Fraser comes to
feel defeated by "hostile circumstances without and a hostile,
senseless nature of his own within." His spirit, "meant to be

free, struggled in vain against the bonds of fate..." (116f.).[30]
Fraser's conviction that "within him lay the power to break
the spell" (117) is itself a product of his romantic imagination,
but one begins to sense the inherent logic in it, for all its sentimentality. He *must* thrust himself into a romantic dream world.
The nearest such world is Beaumont. "Castles and dragons.
That is what young men in love demand," Colonel Prevost tells
Fraser toward the end of the war. "This has been a castle for
you" (406).

Boyd controlled the point of view in the novel firmly enough
to reveal both Fraser's romantic consciousness and the inherent
misconceptions that proceed from it. Fraser judges a tourna-
ment he watches from a distance at Beaumont to be "a curious
performance, affected, [and] dandified" but "somehow stirring" (53). And precisely because it and the world it belongs
to are stirring, Fraser has to seek the hand of Stewart Prevost,
although the spectacle of a "back-country boy in cow-hide
brogans calling on the Colonel's daughter" (120f.) is grotesque,
as he himself recognizes. Fraser's ambivalence, however, does
not imply that two real options are available. In effect, there
is only one context in which his spiritual ideal may be pursued.
His quest for the beautiful maiden is metaphoric. Stewart Prevost functions as an ideal for Fraser much as Daisy Buchanan
does for Jay Gatsby in F. Scott Fitzgerald's *The Great Gatsby*.[31]

A complex of factors, therefore, leads Fraser to seek Stewart
Prevost and to commit himself to the Confederate cause even
though it is not in his best interest to do so. The war gave back
to the poor white, Boyd said, "in his own eyes and the eyes of
his folks, a validity so long denied him by the planters that he
had ceased to believe in it himself."[32] Essentially, Fraser is
duped into supporting the plantation aristocracy, the most
grandiose illusion of all, because it seems to be the only possible
context for humane existence. In fighting for it, he helps sustain the very structure that robs him of his humanity. His
commitment to the war is essentially suicidal, and its tragic
circularity is a major motif in the novel. As four Negroes unload
a case of rifles from a river barge at the Prevost plantation,
Fraser notices that it takes on "more than ever the aspect of
a coffin" (202).

The war carries to its logical conclusion every illusion and
misconception implicit in the plantation system; it completes

the destruction of the land and the degradation of the human spirit. Its awful logic and fateful continuity become concrete in the metaphor of the marching that finally strips the men free from the land itself and expels the spirit from their bodies. At first, mind and spirit resist the punishment the body has to endure (271), but soon the men merely move woodenly, "their spirits tortured and driven by the spell" (317). Finally, like "lost souls doomed to stumble through a never-ending hell of weariness" (326), they march through "a vastly tortured fantasy performed by disembodied spirits" (331). When Fraser's company is finally captured, the men find not relief but more marching in the arid silence of a Dantean hell "beyond fear, beyond sense, beyond existence" (356f.).

Before James Fraser ever reaches the prison, he is becoming a "lean and dusty wolf-man, ravenous in body and in spirit" (320). For most of the men, degradation of spirit is completed by atavistic degeneration of body in the primeval, infernolike conditions of the prison: "Among the mounds, the holes, the mud, crept shapes, dark, silent, moving slowly...." When a new man enters, "gray cadavers ... [rear up] on their haunches ... with eyes like stones, deep-set, inscrutable as death" (357f.). The war that was begun to preserve the power of the Prevosts, with their "fine-cut" aristocratic faces (49), has brought about a state of existence in which only the obscene Racker twins, with their "rat-like smiles" (217), are at home.

After his exchange (through the rather improbable influence of Colonel Prevost), Fraser returns to Beaumont to claim Stewart's hand. Prevost, mellowed by the war and true to his aristocratic code ("I found that my daughter had given her heart to you. That left me no alternative."), consents to the marriage (408), which symbolically completes the replacement of an aristocratic society by a democratic one. In the conventional historical romance, the lowborn suitor is frequently denied the hand of his fair lady until it has been accidentally discovered that he himself is of noble birth. Nothing of the kind happens in *Marching On*; what we have is two people whose union is possible only through the destruction of what each of them was before and of the very condition of society that created an artificial chasm between them. The irony is that James Fraser fought in the war against that which he desired above all else— a chance to move across class lines as a human being.

The Fraser-Prevost romance is a tactical error in *Marching On*; but, since it is consistent with the historical and psychological Realism that is basic to the novel, it is not a strategic blunder. "It don't seem natural to have you here in this house of ours," James tells Stewart after their marriage. "I used to make pictures of myself going to Beaumont. But I never figured about you coming here" (418). The leveling is downward, not upward. As Robert A. Lively says, the defeat of the Prevost system "was more important than true love in bringing the plantation belle to her cornshuck wedding bed."[33]

In 1927, the Civil War novel did not have a particularly distinguished past. Robert A. Lively concludes from a survey of more than five hundred of them that the great mass are "subliterary."[34] Lively rightly deplores, however, the slipshod criticism that has perpetuated stereotypes which bear little resemblance to the actual novels. He argues, for instance, that the "extravagant [critical] emphasis on . . . partisan feeling" in the novels is without foundation, for the single most persistent theme in them is actually the *reconciliation* of opposed loyalties.[35] The Civil War novel, however, has been neither a unified nor a static tradition. The "modern" Civil War novel was born in the mid-1920's,[36] inaugurating a "wave" that Bernard DeVoto saw as the fourth in our literary history, distinguished from the novels of earlier waves by greater historical realism, psychological validity, and social awareness.[37] To a degree, these qualities had been present in some earlier Civil War novels; it is their union in a single novel, in conjunction with an economic interpretation of the causes of the war, that marks a Civil War novel as "new." There was also a change in scale and a coincident change in focus. Novelists who focused on the grand panorama of the conflict were replaced by those who sought to "illuminate cultures through complete understanding of [particular] persons within them."[38]

Changes in the Civil War novel derived partially from changing opinions among historians. Thomas J. Pressly has shown that, before 1880, explanations of the causes of the war originated with partisans of either the North or the South, or with individuals such as Clement Vallandigham of Ohio who insisted it was caused by "artificial issues . . . emotionalized by zealots."[39] Later, James Ford Rhodes, Frederick Jackson Turner, and others suggested it was an "irrepressible conflict" caused by such "in-

animate forces" as geography and economics. Views on the war
held by early twentieth-century historians have differed sharply,
but perhaps most influential was the economic one of Charles
A. Beard, to whom it was a "Second American Revolution."[40]

Although *Marching On* appeared too early to be influenced by
Beard, its economic orientation suggests that Boyd's view of
the war was a modern one—possibly a synthesis of Vallandigham's, Rhodes's, and Edward Channing's (Channing published
his *The War for Southern Independence* in 1925). The Civil
War, Boyd later said, "far from being irrepressible . . . [was]
synthetically manufactured over an issue that was in danger
of being settled peacefully" through moral suasion and economic necessity.[41] This view is essentially the one presented
in the novel.

So far as the novelist was concerned, Boyd said war could
no longer be presented "as a romantic mythology of Knights
and heroes"; war novels must rest on fact. In 1925, ascertaining
those facts was not easy, since treatises on the war in the South
and on southern life of the period were still relatively few.
Francis Pendleton Gaines's *The Southern Plantation* appeared
in 1925, but the major work of Ulrich B. Phillips was still a
decade away; and major southern collections of archival materials
were just being assembled. As a result, Boyd worked primarily
with published, official documents; with nineteenth-century
diaries, journals, and memoirs; and with the imaginative literature of the period of Cooke, Timrod, Hayne, Legaré, Simms,
Lanier, and others.

As primary historical sources, he used the North Carolina
legislative archives, newspapers, the one-hundred-and-thirty-
volume *Official Records of the Rebellion,* the published correspondence of Civil War governor Zebulon B. Vance, and collections of proslavery tracts in the state library. These were
supplemented by such diaries, journals, and memoirs as Sir
Charles Lyell's *Travels in North America* (1845), Frederick
Law Olmstead's *A Journey Through the Seaboard Slave States*
(1856) and *A Journey in the Back Country* (1860), the memoirs
of Jefferson Davis, J. B. Jones's *A Rebel War Clerk's Diary*
(1866), and Thomas W. Higginson's *Army Life in a Black
Regiment* (1870).

Boyd used his materials with considerable care (his card for
H. J. Eckenrode's book on Jefferson Davis notes simply, "Nordic

nonsense"), but in general his research for *Marching On* was less extensive than for *Drums,* partially because there is less attempt to integrate the protagonist's actions and major historical events, and partially because the characters are more imaginative creations than historical figures who had to be "accurately" drawn. Colonel Prevost is in some respects similar to Edmund Ruffin (about whom Boyd read a good deal), but the two figures are in no sense actual counterparts.

By focusing on the middle and lower classes, as both his research and the novel show that he did, Boyd took a realistic approach to the war which was not to be finally established in Civil War novels for some time. Ellen Glasgow's *The Battle Ground* (1902) and Tom Watson's *Bethany* (1904) both suggest the possibilities of treating the war realistically, but focusing on the middle and lower classes did not make "objective Realists" of the Civil War novelists who followed them. Robert Lively argues persuasively that most of them were led by Agrarian sympathies to treat the yeoman farmer idealistically.[42] Contending that most of the novelists "accepted in varying degrees the habits of rural life, if not the formal principles of Agrarian philosophy," Lively argues that they "usually [took] their sectional viewpoints from the traditions of the area in which they were born." This fact, he says, was more important than "attention to scholarly method" in writing the novels. For such writers as Andrew Lytle and Stark Young, the argument is valid; but for Boyd it is neither convincing in terms of the novel itself nor valid biographically.

Lively pictures Boyd as a fox-hunting southerner who built his home "as a replica of William Byrd's Westover."[43] The fact is, however, that Boyd was by ancestry and birth a northerner; he spent relatively little time in the South until after he was grown, and he never established permanent residence there until he was past thirty years old (see Chapter 1). Whether his dual relationship with the North and South actually produced his ambivalent point of view is open to question, but the fact is that his allegiance lay wholly with neither the South, which he once called "a high type of primitive civilization," nor with the North, which was by comparison "a low type of more advanced civilization."[44]

In the early 1920's Boyd knew some of the writers (having talked with them at Paul Green's home in Chapel Hill) who later declared themselves to be Agrarians, and the agrarian theme had been growing in southern historical scholarship since the turn of the century;[45] but there is, in fact, no Agrarianism in *Marching On*. Instead, there is a harsh Naturalism. In *Drums*, the Little River farm of Johnny Fraser was too restrictive to contain his romantic spirit, but its lush protectiveness provided psychological and physical refuge, nevertheless; James Fraser's farm does neither. Instead, it suggests the general hostility of nature to people of his class for whom hope lies not on the farm but in the roundhouse at Wilmington. The forbidden world of Beaumont is presently closed to Fraser, and it is ultimately doomed for everyone. The first railroad worker he sees in Wilmington, a brakeman, appears to him as "an Olympian figure" (134).

Two final strictures that Lively enters against the Civil War novels of the 1920's and 1930's must be examined briefly in relationship to *Marching On*.[46] Following DeVoto's suggestion, Lively says that the Agrarian commitment prevented novelists from examining the middle class with the absolute fidelity to historical fact that their competence in the methods of Realism should allow, and from treating the lowest class (the "dirt eaters" and "resin suckers") at all.[47] Second, he asserts that historical Realism, insofar as it is employed, paradoxically obligates the novelist "to state arguments in terms which reflect the views of the participants," and therefore prevents him from analyzing the period "in the light of his knowledge of the struggle's eventual meaning."[48]

The omission of the "crackers" from Civil War novels which develop in terms of economic motives and class consciousness is, even in the abstract, a minor defect (as Lively himself recognizes). Suffice it to say, however, that the class is not omitted in *Marching On*. Members of the Scroggs family play a relatively minor part in the novel, but the bestial Racker twins are more important, probably as important as the statistical incidence of the class in the 1860's could justify. We are very much aware of both planters and "crackers" in the novel, but we are even more cognizant that the Frasers and their like are at the center of the drama, as indeed they should be.

The question of the novelist's ability to assess the meaning of the war is at least as important, and more complex, than that of his handling of the details of class structure. In support of his statement concerning the Civil War novelists' failure in that respect, Lively adduces a speech by Major Cassius Pettibone in *Marching On*: "The Yankee, seh, can be explained in just one word and in only one.... Money. Money, by God, seh!... And on top of that he preaches abolition at us.... Do you want to know what the Yankee's motto is? It's money for himself and morality for everybody else" (160f.). The explanation is simplistic, Lively charges: to come to terms "with recent economic views [on the causes and meaning of the war] the novelist would have to divorce his history from his fiction."[49] Lively's conclusion itself is simplistic, however, because it disregards the novelist's ability to control point of view, and through it, tone.

At the time Pettibone makes his speech to Fraser on the Yankee venality and hypocrisy that he believes is leading to war, he had already been presented as a windy, self-deluded politician. "Well, seh," he says to Fraser, "during my fo'ty years in politics, where I hope I was happy enough not to disappoint the flattering confidence of my constituents, I observed the Yankees mighty close. And though now retired, I trust not without honor, certainly not without a gratifying token of esteem, I refer, seh, to the clock, which now adorns my parlor mantelpiece and, striking every hour, reminds me of my generous suppo'ters" (160). Pettibone then proceeds to make the observation that Lively quotes, which clearly cannot be taken at face value; indeed, Boyd makes sure it is not. Cynically patronized by Pettibone as one of the "skilled mechanics ... [to whom] we shall owe our prosperity," Fraser acquires "a new idea of his own dignity and broad historical significance." He had always thought, the narrator says, that he had gone to the railroad shops for practical reasons—to get away from home, to make some money, perhaps to advance himself. "But there was evidently more to it," Fraser begins to think, "[he] was one on whom the leaders like Major Pettibone relied, to whom they gave their respect as to a man who had gallantly ... chosen a calling which would lead the South to new ... achievement" (165). The disingenuous tone evokes only sympathy for Fraser and contempt for Pettibone. The whole episode is explicitly ironic.

As in *Drums,* there is a sense of history operating in *Marching On*. We see not only how the conflict was understood at the time by southerners but also in what sense their understanding was deficient, and how the deficiencies explain the "rise

CHAPTER 4

Two Novels of the Frontier:
Long Hunt and *Bitter Creek*

ONE of the more memorable scenes in *Drums* is the final one. Johnny Fraser watches General Greene's army march through the forest past his home in the Little River country. At the rear of the column a solitary scout, "a tall, half-naked mountain man," pauses at the top of a knoll and looks back. Fraser raises a stiff arm in salutation; and, in reply, the "distant figure [lifts] a long black rifle against the sunset sky." The mountaineer "man against the sky" reappears in *Marching On* in the one company of James Fraser's regiment that has retained a sense of its separateness and unity: "A company of lean and long-haired mountaineers from Mitchell [County], who clung tenaciously to their coonskin caps, disdaining to talk to low-landers, disdaining to drink the lowland water, squatted aloof and silent before their tents, their hawklike faces turned toward the horizon as though they hoped to catch a glimpse of the Unakas or hear the tinkle of the springs on Grandfather [Mountain]."[1]

Boyd told Maxwell Perkins that his first impulse when he finished *Marching On* was to write a third novel of historical incident, perhaps a war novel. By early fall of 1927, however, he had focused not on a specific historical incident but on a character whose state of mind was characteristic of a certain period in American history, whose life was governed by a particular set of historical conditions, but whose actions were unrelated to any identifiable historical event. The character who presented himself was the mountaineer who raised his rifle in salute to Johnny Fraser and who, disdaining to share the companionship of James Fraser and his lowland companions, silently scorned the rigid rows of canvas tents, rolled up in his blanket

87

and went to sleep. "I'd like to take a N. C. pioneer of either the
late colonial or early Am. period," Boyd told Perkins, "No Fraser
but a lewd ignorant brave restless fellow cunning in woodcraft
& sly & stupid about all else. . . ."[2] This is the first sketch of
Murfree Rinnard in *Long Hunt,* certainly one of the most coherent and compelling of all Boyd's characters.

I Long Hunt (*1930*)

Boyd himself felt that *Long Hunt* was the best of his first
three novels, and his feeling was shared by some of his most
sensitive readers.[3] *Long Hunt* went on sale April 4, 1930; about
sixteen thousand copies were sold during the first four months,
which was about equal to the sale of *Drums,* but somewhat less
than that of *Marching On.*

In Hill Town, North Carolina, near the end of the eighteenth
century, sixteen-year-old Laurel leans against a fence and scans
the trail leading to the mountains, watching for the long hunters
who come to town each spring to sell their pelts, spend their
money for women and liquor, reoutfit, and return to the forest.
Only faintly aware of her "tawny and seductive" womanly ripe-
ness, Laurel simply wishes innocently for relief from the oppressive dullness of the settlement.[4]

From a gap in the mountains, tall, hard-eyed, Murfree Rinnard starts down into the settlement, moving with the wiry
grace of an Indian. As he enters town, he feels the houses "close
around him"; but he stays awhile because the hunting season is
over and he wants to "take another look" at Laurel, whom he
had seen briefly on his last trip. Rinard spends several weeks in
Hill Town, alternately carousing with his uncouth friends at
Major Tyrell's tavern and visiting Laurel. Eventually he tries to
seduce her, as he has so many women before; is shamed and
angered by her confused resistance; and visits immediately the
more complaisant half-breed girls of the town. Later, when he
returns penitent to Laurel, she accepts his rather hesitant proposal of marriage. But on the night before the wedding, he
flees to the forest again, goes to Nashville, and contracts to hunt
bear for fur-trader Hoffman. Months later he seduces Ann Walden, who reminds him of Laurel, and flees again, this time to
Natchez.

After a mission into Indian country for the governor of the

Mississippi Territory, Rinnard returns to Nashville and hears the news of Laurel's marriage. For the next seven years, he lives among Upper Creek Indians, but he returns finally to visit her. Seeing her aged and worn is such a traumatic experience that he flees without speaking. Hearing later that the settlement where Laurel lives is under siege by the Indians, he goes to help; and his sense of guilt prompts him to make a successful but suicidal attempt to bring water into the fort.

Reviewers recognized that *Long Hunt* had to be judged by somewhat different criteria than those employed for *Drums* and *Marching On,* which were clearly historical novels that were superior to most earlier novels of the type. But *Long Hunt* is both a historical novel and a Realistic, psychological novel. As a Realistic novel, it is not without defect. Allan Nevins found *Long Hunt* deficient in "living characters," including Rinnard, but successful in conveying the "essence of history" without employing "raw historical fact."[5] John Chamberlain, who was more precise than Nevins in his enthusiasms and in his reservations regarded *Long Hunt* as lying between the "purely pictorial" values of Winston Churchill's *The Crossing* (1904) and the "human and poetic" values of Elizabeth M. Roberts's *The Great Meadow* (1930).[6] *Long Hunt* is "far from dependent of the romantic props of *The Crossing*," Chamberlain said, "but it is, in spite of its vivid realism . . . a more romantic and a more sentimental work than *The Great Meadow*," primarily because Rinnard's vision of Laurel remains "too unconscionably long."[7] His reservations notwithstanding, Chamberlain saw more clearly than most other reviewers that Rinnard is caught in a twofold tragedy. His long hunts provide the only apparent escape but no actual refuge from the vision of Laurel, and in the end his way of life as a long hunter is doomed.

Rinnard has every reason to feel threatened by the squalid, crooked row of "slab roofs and clay-daubed chimneys." His solitary rambles through the virgin forests beyond the mountains have been broken only by intervals of indulgence with the liquor and with the crude half-breed women of the trading posts. He is confident that "there never was, and never would be any one better able to live his own life"; and he is also secure in the knowledge that he has "never missed a [woman] that he'd really tried" (27) nor allowed any of them to get the slightest hold on him.

Nevertheless, he senses Laurel's strange power. He is familiar with the response her physical attractiveness produces in him, but her spiritual purity is alien. Rinnard senses that Laurel lives "in a higher world" and that he himself is "a hard-bitten mortal listening with . . . awe to the prattlings of a holy child" (73). He wants to carry her "up the mountainside, beyond the town lights" and to make her the goddess of the holy place which is the unspoiled wilderness (82).

Rinnard's intention to marry Laurel lasts less than a day. He remembers the married long hunters he has known, "cluttered up with wife and children," scratching out a living on a half-cleared farm. Through his window at night he sees the stars "clear as silver rifle sights" (89) and feels the west wind on his face. Before dawn he is on his way to the wilderness beyond the mountain, pausing momentarily before the small house where Laurel sleeps, but stopping only when he stands "astride his world, his rifle in his hand," at the top of the mountain (100). Free from "the close-built walls, the smells, the talk, the trading; the land of penned shoats tromping their own mire" (100), Rinnard beds down: "[The] mountain night was cold. The stars snapped hard and sharp. The stream below gave out an icy tinkle. But under the cedar he was bedded warm. . . . All [was] warm and quiet." (96).

But Rinnard still has three lessons to learn about the world he lives in. The first he learns almost immediately; the second takes a little longer; and the final one nearly ten years. Each one makes it clearer that the freedom he seeks is incompatible with the security he demands. The first lesson is a clear paradox: he and the other long hunters form the vanguard of a host of "greedy, smelly, loud-mouthed men" who are cutting up the western wilderness into "truck patches and hog lots" (123). Rinnard does his part by guiding the settler Ed Walden and his family into Tennessee. Unwilling to share the guilt, Rinnard decides the spoiling of the wilderness is "all the fault of the movers"; but his own complicity is ultimately inescapable.

While the wilderness still exists, however, Rinnard lives by its predatory laws, particularly where women are concerned. When his hunting companion tells him he has been chasing whores so long he does not know anything else, he replies: "I've chased anything that took my fancy, and the only difference is, you don't have to give presents to some" (221). But Rinnard's cyn-

icism is merely a mask for his inability to face a more fundamental difference. The faded but elegant whore Mrs. Brattles,
who he thinks is "surely the highest toned piece he [has] ever
had in all his frolicking" (182), satisfies his physical lust but
leaves him spiritually empty. Rinnard at first feels the emptiness in only a visceral way, but it is persistent and ultimately
more compelling than his need for crude physical pleasures.
Moreover, he feels that the emptiness can be filled only by a
woman—and therein lies the difficulty.

On a literal level, Rinnard believes that "of all encumbrances,
women [are] the worst" (128). No long hunter could allow
himself to settle into a nest with a woman, whose very nature
commits her to all of those things of which his own life is a
symbolic rejection. Unfortunately, he finds them fatally attractive, possessed of a "soft and secret power ... against his freedom" (232). That power acts to involve him in the life of
another person, and he fears involvement more than anything
else (254). His most dramatic flight from involvement is his
escape from Ann Walden who is an obvious surrogate for Laurel.

Rinnard fears Laurel more than any other woman; he avoids
thinking about her for fear that "the shadow of her power might
fall on him again" (232f.). But Ann is attractive to him precisely
because she resembles Laurel, although he rationalizes his attach-
ment to her in other terms. "The more women with loving hearts
a man could find," he tells himself, "the less he would be in
the power of any one" (233). The result of Rinnard's cynical
liaison with Ann is paradoxically not to free him of Laurel's
power but to reinforce it. He can literally pry Ann's hands
loose from him as he escapes down the river, but he cannot escape
Laurel's hold on his mind. Her grip on him finally drives him
into the desperate frenzy of a trapped animal. In one of his
encampments on his way to Natchez, a racoon that gets caught
in one of his traps raises "two black pleading hands" (256), but
Rinnard kills it in a symbolic gesture of hatred for the pleading
passivity of all creatures who compromise their vicious instinct
for freedom.

In Natchez, Rinnard meets Monsieur de Milo, who describes
himself immodestly but more or less accurately as "a citizen
of the world, a natural philosopher, and a man who understands
women" (272). Milo undertakes to explain Rinnard's predica-
ment: "You were confronted with a dilemma, and ... you made

the obvious, if not the most daring, choice. You knew the worth
of freedom and decided to keep that, rather than change it for
the unknown." Rinnard cannot comprehend Milo's assertion
that freedom is mainly a state of mind (279); he knows only
that he feels trapped by the vision of Laurel, which returns
with increasing frequency, and that the hard savagery of the
women of the towns and trading posts neither assuages his real
hunger nor dispels the vision.

Monsieur de Milo is only partially correct when he tells Rinnard that a man "can never resist a woman who loves him for
an attribute he does not possess" (271f.). The paradoxical fact
is that Rinnard has always had the same fatal attractiveness for
women that Laurel has for him. He is caught in a trap of his
own construction because Laurel, being so different from the
other women, has become for him "other," has failed to fit
into his normal frame of reference. His freedom, being primarily
spiritual, had been immune to threats by sensual, spiritless
creatures. But Laurel is both body and spirit, and Rinnard cannot escape the picture of her "standing by the paling fence
with her copper hair around her eyes, waiting for him to come"
(333). She alone seems real.

Although Rinnard does not realize it, Laurel has been from
the beginning a kind of Beatrice whose mission is to lead him
beyond the hell of his own passions. Early in the novel, she leads
him to the Spruce Grove above the town: "The moon rode
steadily against a tide of wind-spun clouds, the sycamores
clicked their branches and threw slow-swinging hatchings along
the whiteness of the road. Her smooth long strides... [fell]
in airy puffs of dust.... When her cloak blew... back, she
seemed like a ship's high riding figurehead.... On up the ridge.
Into the shadows... the secret sounds of the mountain" (58f.).
Later, Rinnard's mind slips back to that image again and again
(150). His flight is almost Augustinian: "Sometimes he felt that
she pursued him. But at other times it seemed as though he pursued her and that at every new place she was already there and
waiting for him" (258).

When Rinnard decides after his seven-year exile to make a
"last accounting with his dreams," he finds Laurel's house "a
meagre shabby lump of varied browns, the brown of pine bark
and of clay and of cypress shingles." In front of the door "a
sickly crepe myrtle [shows] yellow leaves." He had hoped

that the sight of her face, "deadened by work and smoke and sun," would free him of the vision; but he finds that her altered physical appearance does not change the essential truth about her (345ff.). Her ideal beauty remains, and finally compels his commitment. The final vision Rinnard has, just before he dies of the wound he receives in his sacrificial attempt to save Laurel and her family, is of "copper and gold . . . through the mist" (376). It suggests that he has finally achieved peace with himself and spiritual union with Laurel.

Boyd's move away from actual historical events as the base of the novel, which began in *Marching On,* continued in *Long Hunt.* It is a historical novel in the sense that its protagonist lives in a remote but authentically re-created era, but the protagonist's story is not in any sense dependent upon actual historical events—particularly dramatic and pivotal ones such as wars. There are, as a matter of fact, no identifiable historical incidents or persons in *Long Hunt.*[8] There are also a few surprising errors of historical fact in the novel. The town of Winston-Salem (83), for instance, did not exist in the early nineteenth century.[9] But such errors actually make little difference in *Long Hunt,* although they would have made a great deal in *Drums* or *Marching On.*

Murfree Rinnard's drama is essentially self-defining; it does not depend for credibility upon a related pattern of historical events. Once the general character and tone of life on the Tennessee frontier during the first decade of the nineteenth century is established—and of course maintained by realistic detail— the "historical" problem is solved. The events of the novel are the events of Murfree Rinnard's life, not those of North Carolina and Tennessee history.

Boyd did historical research for *Long Hunt,* but he did less of it by far than he had for the earlier novels. He seems to have used extensively only three historical sources: William Winterbotham's *An Historical . . . View of the American United States* (1795), James Hall's *Brief History of the Mississippi Territory* (1801), and André Michaux's *Travels to the West of the Alleghany Mountains* (1802). The research file for *Long Hunt* is minute in comparison with those for the earlier novels. Categories such as "politics," which had many entries for *Drums,* have disappeared, suggesting the change in emphasis.

In the earlier novels, Boyd achieved historical authenticity partially by relying on an accurate time structure (coherent both internally and externally), precisely located and fully described geographical settings, and a pattern of identifiable historical events and characters. In *Long Hunt,* however, time is defined only in broad terms (ca. 1799-1810); the topography of Rinnard's wilderness is fully described, but in such as way as to produce immediate realism rather than historical "setting" in the conventional sense; historical characters and events are entirely absent. The one historical issue present is historical in broad terms only: the inherent paradoxes of the American mind and its relation to the paradoxes of the frontier in American history.

Since the issue has been examined repeatedly by American writers, it is not surprising that Murfree Rinnard's ancestors are more literary than historical. In Boyd's research file there are many references to Davy Crockett's *Narrative* (1834), and in Rinnard's recollection of one of his periodic revels is more than an echo of William Gilmore Simms and Augustus Baldwin Longstreet: "He had been half cocked on Hoffman's liquor most of the time, and more than that some of the time. He had drunk and sung and frolicked and played cards . . . and slept snug with [his dog] under Hoffman's counter, and one night he had beat a man from the cave country of Kentucky at throwing the tomahawk at a mark on [the] door, and when the constable had come, they had pulled his shirt over his head and trussed him up. After that, he was top dog among the Tennessee boys in town" (182f.). Whatever else he is, Rinnard is a link in the long chain of ring-tailed roarers. We also find elements of native American humor throughout the novel, as well as plot devices, characters, and idiomatic usages that have recognizable antecedents in such humorists as Artemus Ward, Josh Billings, and Petroleum V. Nasby (cf. 34ff.).

Rinnard's most important literary ancestor is Natty Bumppo. James Fenimore Cooper was not the first to recognize the crisis of consciousness that was associated with the steady recession of the frontier,[10] but that crisis achieved in Natty Bumppo what is still its fullest and most characteristic expression. Natty is the paradigmatic type of all those who discover in themselves the intolerable but unavoidable attraction for both nature and civilization.[11] Murfree Rinnard's characteristic pose "astride his world" in *Long Hunt* has antecedents not only in *Drums* and

Marching On but also in Cooper's *The Pioneers* and *The Prairie*:
"The sun had fallen below the crest of the nearest wave of the
prairie.... In the centre of this flood of fiery light a human
form appeared.... The figure was colossal: the attitude musing
and melancholy.... But imbedded, as it was, in its setting of
garish light, it was impossible to distinguish its just proportions
or true character."[12]

But Rinnard differs in several respects from Natty Bumppo
and, in doing so, achieves his own unique identity. Natty is
so idealized, not to say sentimentalized,[13] that readers of modern Realistic fiction often find it difficult to respond to him as
a real man acting in the real world. Boyd had the advantage of
writing after the Realistic movement was established, however,
and thus had options in dealing with the nature versus civilization problem that were not open to Cooper. Although Murfree
Rinnard's problem is precisely Natty Bumppo's, he is modeled
as a character not only on Bumppo but also on Davy Crockett,
Mike Fink, and Joe Meek.[14] What Rinnard loses in epic stature,
he makes up in multidimensional Realism as a character. Rinnard's world of nature is also Bumppo's, but the people who
inhabit that world are more realistically defined than the light
and dark maidens and antiseptic Indians of Cooper's Genessee
River country. Even the crude but relatively respectable Billy
Kirby of *The Pioneers* is replaced by such thoroughly rustic
characters as Hoffman, Major Tyrell, Isoceles Bagg, and old
man Widden—all of whom owe their existence far more to Twain
and the southwestern humorists than to Cooper.

Boyd was not alone in recognizing that developments in literary technique allowed the problem of Natty and his counterparts
to be treated freshly in a way that would be valid for readers
attuned to psychological Realism as a fictional mode. Elizabeth
Madox Roberts's *The Great Meadow,* also published in 1930,
received by and large more favorable reviews than *Long Hunt*.
Since *The Great Meadow* is still often assumed to be the best
restatement of the frontier theme in fiction of the 1930's, it might
be useful to compare the two novels briefly.

Superficially, *Long Hunt* and *The Great Meadow* strongly
resemble each other. Both are set in the closing years of the
eighteenth century and in the opening years of the nineteenth;
both have the same general subject; both are primarily concerned with the relationship of men to the land they inhabit;

both are in a sense historical novels.[15] But their differences are ultimately more important than their similarities, and the most important difference is that *The Great Meadow* has a female protagonist and is told from a feminine point of view. The main interest for Diony Hall is to domesticate the wilderness, to settle into a nest, and she shares that interest with virtually everyone else in the novel, the men included. As Berk Jarvis woos her in her home in Virginia, he tells her they will go "to the country behind the mountains and start a new world there."[16] They proceed to do precisely that, possessing themselves of the land "by the power of their courage, their order, and their endurance" (168). But to possess the land is not to apprehend it in its infinite freedom, as it was for Murfree Rinnard. The vision of Diony and Berk Jarvis is a vision "of stone walls and rail fences setting bounds to the land, making contentment and limitations for the mind to ease itself upon," and causing the "wearying infinitives of the wilderness [to] come to an end" (208f.).

Paradoxically, their life in the new world demands that they accept voluntary servitude to the comfortable and comforting spaces they have created. There is something pathetic in Murfree Rinnard's counterpart Evan Muir, married to Diony after Berk's presumed death, standing "vaguely servile before the greatness of the house and humble beside the large hearthstone" (296). The hearthstone clearly symbolizes Diony's vision, and that of all women before her who habitually equate a nest for the body with a home for the mind. Diony has a sense of herself "as eternal, as if all that she did now were of a kind older than kings, older than beliefs and governments" (254). She is, after all, named for the mythic Dione; she sees her brothers as "earth-men, delving in the soil to make it yield bread" (14f.).

Murfree Rinnard is the eternally restless male, moving perpetually toward the receding frontiers of the mind. *Long Hunt* is more powerful than *The Great Meadow*, not simply because it employs a male protagonist and is impelled to action by the male vision, but because it contains in Laurel the feminine vision as well and can therefore take its energy from the tension between two opposed points of view and modes of action in the world. The actual difference between Diony's vision and Berk's or Evan Muir's is slight; the difference between Laurel's and Rinnard's is nearly polar. This is not to say that Laurel and

Rinnard do not share aspects of each other's vision; indeed they do, and in the sharing lies the essential tragedy of the novel. But each is drawn fatally toward the other because the other is finally so different from himself. The hope of resolution, not to say salvation, is for each to learn to trust himself to "go by contraries," as the protagonists of Frost's "West-running Brook" learn. At the end of *Long Hunt*, Rinnard implicitly names the day of his death the "day of what we *both* said."

The weakness of *The Great Meadow* is that there is only one point of view, one vision of the world. Paradoxically, the logic of that vision should cause Diony to stay in the comfortable nest already made for her in Albemarle County, Virginia. The push beyond the mountains comes, not because it is demanded by the qualities of her own mind, but because it happened in American history. Murfree Rinnard and the girl Laurel represent the archetypal forces of a continuing historical process; Diony Hall and Berk Jarvis and Evan Muir are pawns in a pattern of historical events that is already complete.

II Bitter Creek (*1939*)

During the summer of 1908, between his sophomore and junior years at Princeton, Boyd took a pack-horse trip through the West. From Billings, Montana, he wrote to his parents:

Fred [Osborn] and I took horses and made for a large butte just the other side of the Yellowstone river. . . . We neared the top and in another instant burst into our first real sight of the West. At our feet the Yellowstone rolled along and we could see it weaving its way down the great valley shining in and out among the dark woods along its banks, while all around stretched the cracked alkali plains and buttes and far far off veiled in the blue haze, rose . . . the sombre snow capped Rockies. We sat silent in our saddles grinning for the pure joy of it. . . . Somehow the [railroad] car seemed squalid, the talk silly after that great broad sight.[17]

After *Drums*, *Marching On*, and *Long Hunt*, Boyd had turned to another type of material for *Roll River* (1935);[18] but he returned about 1936 to the motifs and themes of *Long Hunt* for a novel about another frontier—the one he had seen in 1908.[19] Boyd's actual progress on the novel was slowed by frequent illnesses and by his collaboration during early 1937 with Paul Green on a play; but by November, 1938, *Bitter Creek* was

finished. It went on sale in the spring of 1939.[20] Sales the first
month after publication amounted to thirteen thousand copies,
which compared favorably with the best sales of the first four
novels.

Nearly three years before *Bitter Creek* was published, Ber-
nardo DeVoto had suggested that, despite the intrinsic attractiveness of the cowboy and his position as the "final" inheritor
of the crucial role once filled by the long hunter, no one but
Eugene Manlove Rhodes and Conrad Richter had yet begun
to realize the subject's literary potential.[21] The essential question for reviewers of *Bitter Creek* was whether Boyd's novel
had made a fresh thing out of the usually sterile Romantic conventions of the "Western." Horace Reynolds of the New York
Times Book Review noted that its elements of conventional
romance and adventure were "tempered by thought, formed and
expressed with reserve and skill."[22] Another reviewer praised
the "almost poetic" style of the novel;[23] and, when Carl Van
Doren published his history of the American novel the following
year, he called *Bitter Creek* "a novel . . . which transcends the
standard westerns."[24]

DeVoto dissented. Boyd's tendency to employ certain Romantic conventions in his earlier novels had not been particularly
damaging, DeVoto suggested; in one or two cases (as in *Roll
River*), it had actually been of positive value because the convention had been employed "in the service of reality." In *Bitter
Creek*, however, the conventions had neither been avoided nor
made functional.[25] Perhaps because he was not thoroughly
familiar with the conventions, a reviewer of the British edition
of *Bitter Creek* the following year found the characters and
incidents not sterile at all, but possessed of a "subtle and quick-
ened humanity." There is, he said, "something of universal
experience in the pattern of their lives."[26]

The questions raised by the reviews need to be settled. How
well does *Bitter Creek* succeed in its own terms? How successful is it in comparison with Boyd's earlier novels? How far does
it go toward either making something fresh and useful of the
sterile conventions of the Western, or setting them aside altogether? Is there, in fact, a universal dimension to the characters,
action, and themes of the novel? Does it belong with novels of
the West that have examined the mythic possibilities of their
subject?

Bitter Creek is set in the Wyoming Territory during the 1870's and 1880's. Ray Talcott is the thirteen-year-old son of a Twin Forks, Illinois, hardware-store owner. After his mother runs away with a hardware salesman to escape her husband's inhumane treatment, Ray finds his own life intolerable. He flees his father's vengeful brutality and suspicion, planning vaguely to "go West." On his way to the rail junction at Kansas City, he meets the malicious Uncle Coon, the sullen and seductive Maribel, the patent-medicine huckster Dr. Antelope, the girl Nancy, the idiot-boy Nolly, and finally, when he boards the train at Kansas City, the free-wheeling cowboy Springtime.

With Springtime, Ray goes to Wyoming and joins an outfit on Bitter Creek. Eleven years pass before his simple and orderly life is interrupted by the arrival of Nancy and Uncle Coon. The lives of people on Bitter Creek become entangled through Uncle Coon's unscrupulous provocation of an Indian war, one resut of which is that Ray marries Nancy, whom he has helped to rescue from the Indians. They live compatibly until a combination of ill fortune, unfounded suspicion, and malevolence separates them temporarily. Through their eventual reconciliation, Ray gains a clearer knowledge of himself and of the mixed motives, cross-purposes, and divided allegiances from which a man must sift meaning for his life.

It is important that *Bitter Creek* does not open with the protagonist already in the West. Nor is he simply moved there coincidentally in order for the story to get underway. Ray Talcott's eventual arrival in the West is the logical result of a carefully delineated psychological conflict. His mother's "light step" and "light voice"[27] provide only momentary relief in the generally forbidding atmosphere dominated by his father, the "spare dark man" (19) with the "cold pale eye" (92). After his mother leaves, Ray's world becomes an intolerable "jumble of frantic and ineffectual shifts to stave off doom" (32). Since he can neither please his father nor defend himself against his malice and brutality, he has but one choice: to flee. In the night he takes the Springfield pike, which he believes leads to the West, to "something far away and free and good" (21). Ray thinks he is escaping the complex frustration and injustices of human society; but during the next few weeks, he actually undergoes a bizarre initiation into its real nature.

Ray's initial conflict is seen against the background of the

Naturalistic Prologue of the novel, which defines the real laws
of human experience, as well as of nature itself. The Prologue
opens upon a paradoxically Romantic natural scene: "The mountains stood up from the plains. Straight up, from shoulders of
dark pines and spruces until their naked tawny sides were lost
in mist. Higher still ... snowfields ... brightened in the light of
the quick rising run. The mist thinned out and trailed away on
airs which drifted into a canyon between two dark rock sides"
(3). The incipient Romantic tone is destroyed, however, by the
appearance of a Piegan Indian who is transporting his household to new hunting grounds. Far from being a Romantic stereotype, the Piegan is merely one link in a Naturalistic cycle of
life: he is hunting the bear which has just gorged himself on
ants that have just raided, with military order and precision, a
nest of hatching fly larvae. The Prologue provides, therefore,
pervasive ironic contrast for any search for certainty, security,
stability, or open-ended freedom in the novel. The story of Ray
Talcott is essentially the story of a naïve young man's initiation
into the mysteries of the predatory Naturalistic cycle that charac-
terizes all experience.

Ray's education in the ways of the world is begun by the
cynical and sadistic Uncle Coon. After hitching a ride on Uncle
Coon's wagon on the first leg of his journey, Ray finds himself
virtually imprisoned for several weeks. Harassed by Uncle Coon,
who watches him constantly with "cruel squirrel eyes" (63), and
bewildered by the vacillatory seductive kindness and hostility
of Coon's niece Maribel, Ray sits on a slab step of the cabin
and watches the moon rise "red and lopsided above the ragged
trees" (33). It is as if the pure malevolence of his father (implicitly the innate evil of the race), embodied in Uncle Coon,
pursues him. At the first opportunity, Ray escapes and continues
his journey westward; but he finds himself almost immediately
hostage again, this time to Dr. Antelope.

Dr. Antelope, who resembles Monsieur de Milo of *Long Hunt,*
is magician, palmist, phrenologist, snake-oil salesman, and ama-
teur philosopher. To Ray's simple question, "Which way are you
heading?," Antelope replies: "From the standpoint of celestial
mechanics ... your question is meaningless. We inhabit an
oblate spheroid. All roads are elliptical and turn in time upon
themselves. However, mundanely speaking, West" (47). Pro-
fessionally, Dr. Antelope is a charlatan, but personally he is a

man of some vision and compassion. Observing with more than
a little irony that candor is the "sacred obligation of true friendship" (52), he teaches Ray during the next few weeks that
human relationships are more often cynical and predatory than
honest and altruistic, that faith in the brotherhood of man is
more of a liability than an asset, that cunning is the first necessity for self-preservation, that appearance and reality are difficult to distinguish, that the world is finally evil, and that most
of the evil is traceable to "good" men.

These being the conditions of life, Antelope tells Ray that
"Adaptability [is] the keystone of the profession" (55). We
understand, of course, that his real profession is life itself. "Look
what the customer gets," he tells Ray of the worthless Navajo
oil, "he gets belief, faith, conviction. The system is automatic
and therefore both infallible and beautiful; unless he has faith
he does not buy the bottle and, since he has faith, the bottle
does him good, all of us being creatures of the mind" (59).
When Uncle Coon appears one evening in the audience of the
medicine show, Ray employs Antelope's adaptability, steals a
pony, and flees.

Soon reduced almost to bestiality by hunger and fatigue, Ray
happens upon some baskets of food stashed under the seats of
buggies drawn up under trees in a churchyard. The Christian
brethren are singing compassionate hymns inside ("I was a
wand'ring sheep . . ."), but Ray quickly learns the real depth
of their Christian compassion. A pious young man sees Ray
prying into the baskets, takes the food from him, and nourishes
him instead with an impromptu sermon on the evils of steal-
ing "while Christian persons are attending worship" (72). The
irony is complete when Ray is subsequently offered both food
and shelter by the idiot-boy Nolly, in whose pagan but compassionate care he learns a final lesson in the ways of the world.

"I ain't the fool they take me for," Nolly tells Ray as he brings
him food in the cave that provides refuge from the malevolence
of "superior" beings (100). Theirs is a fellowship of suffering;
it is the first time Ray has not been used for cynical purposes.
The "green shaded valley" (83) offers rest and security until
the specter of Uncle Coon appears again. With Nolly's help, Ray
escapes and catches a train to Saint Louis and then to Kansas
City, where he meets Springtime.

The "hard-worn elegance" of Springtime's cowboy garb seems

incredibly romantic (107) to Ray, and before long he has accepted an invitation to join the outfit Springtime works for, near Bitter Creek. On the second day of their ride toward the ranch, they cross a river and stop to rest at the top of a small hill. The freedom Ray experiences as he gets his first real view of the West is both literal and metaphoric: "On the left the mountain wall stood up to the center of the sky, on the right the plains lay shining in the light of the bright new sun. . . . High on this tableland, bounded at measureless distance by mountains, plains and sky and sun, he felt his old life very small and faint and far away . . ." (121).

For eleven years Ray's life in the West has an apparent stability and continuity: he rides herd in the spring and fall, hunts during the winter with the Indians, and spends his money on liquor, gambling, and women. The landscape itself is a metaphor for the condition of mind he has come West to find: "Big country; enormous and serene, white snow wall, black pines and faint green floor . . . [with] the pure blue over all" (167). He tells himself that "Nothing [means] anything . . . but the range" (295); all he wants is "To work with cattle and with horses, to do a good hand's job and to feel the mountains and the sky and the ways of other men who lived like him. That was . . . enough for any man" (153).

The activities of Ray's life on the range are themselves actually less important, however, than the insulation against change that they presumably offer. He tells himself that "No man [has] ever seen a finer country" (167) and that his deepest desire is for it "to stay like it was and [himself] to stay in it, like he was" (149). But as his eyes sweep the horizon, he sees the tin roof of a ranch house and a windmill turning awkwardly (167). Eventually, he is forced to admit that "Nothing [stays] still. This life of his [is] changing" (295).

The law of all change, which it takes Ray longer than it should to learn, is that one form of life renews itself by feeding on other forms (165). The Naturalistic cycle introduced by the Prologue and developed in Book I is extended in Book II until it governs not only organic processes but also the racial, economic, social, and historical ones. Animals feed on the land; Indians feed upon animals and the land; the ranchers and nesters prey upon the Indians, animals, and the land; the saloon keepers and prostitutes in town fatten upon the cowboys and the ranchers.

In such a process, a man has two choices: either to change with it, or to be destroyed by it. In this respect, Ray's idyllic hunts with the old Piegan warrior Many Clouds can only be considered anachronistic and neurotic. Ray himself observes, when he helps lead an army detachment against an Indian village to rescue Nancy, that the young warriors are destroyed and left "on a heap like dog-meat bones" where the wolves will get them in the spring, merely because "they had a way of life and could not change it . . . fast enough" (291).

Ray finally has to accept the fact that the West as he has construed it in his own mind is an illusion—its coherence, its stability, its order. "[I] have finally come to the conclusion," says Goggle Jones, who is leaving his job as a bank clerk to go back to school in the East, "that . . . [the West] is an unlimited, a complete, a total fraud. . . . This so-called land of opportunity is chronically broke, chronically inflated, and periodically prostrated by panics, droughts, blizzards, Indian scares and fictitious booms" (367f.).

In his oratorical enthusiasm Jones overstates the case, but his observations are basically correct. The vaunted freedom of the West is an allusion at every level, he asserts: "A cowhand works himself to death for forty dollars, and as the country develops . . . he has less and less chance of rising to the ranks of the doomed cattlemen. . . . [The] lowly homesteader . . . lured on by a spendthrift government and the local boomers, completes the ruin of the cattle business in his march to merited extinction." Democracy in the West, Jones says, "is distinguished by contempt for special ability and intolerance of any other way of life. . . . [The] Westerner is a timid individual who lives in terror of [unfamiliar] ideas. . . ." The final paradox, as Jones sees it, is that the Naturalistic cycle that begins with the land itself ends not in the West but in the hands of eastern investors. If "anything worthwhile should develop here," he concludes, "that is where the profits will go" (368f.).

The West as a complete and self-fulfilling system, or even as a rational and productive system in human terms, is a figment of the Romantic imagination. To make such an assertion, however, is not to dispose of the problem but to come precisely to its crux. Since it does not exist as objective fact, the enigma of the West cannot be solved in the domain of objective fact; it must be solved in that of the imagination. The final problem for Ray Talcott is not historical but spiritual. His involvement with the West is metaphoric as well as actual, and the West itself is only part of the metaphor. The other part is Woman.

Woman is the stubborn fact against which Ray Talcott must always measure his commitments. She is the hub of the wheel of complex circumstance upon which he searches for the elusive, quiet center of both freedom and security. He must continually reassess his past, reinterpret his present, and evaluate his intentions for the future as he encounters the awkward tenderness and passionate fury of Mirabel, the innocent and subtle wiles of the youthful Nancy, the stoic fortitude of the Indian women, the brazen hardness and paradoxical compassion of the prostitute Sue, and finally the wounded, guarded devotion of his wife. Women, as the sardonic Professor Crittenden says, "is a circumstance which alters cases" (205).

Ray spends his share of money on the prostitutes in Greasewood City, but his general attitude toward women verges on paranoia. He fears that his freedom will be infringed or his security intentionally betrayed. Safe momentarily in Nolly's cave on his journey west, he implored the innocent but inquisitive Nancy to take her "Judas Priestly" calf and be gone before someone discovers his hiding place (86). There is "always a catch in women somewhere" (176), Talcott believes; and, although the catch derives more from his attitude than from the intentions or actions of any woman, one fact is clear: women are helping to change the life of the West—the only life he has ever been able to accept.[28]

Talcott finally marries Nancy for a variety of reasons, some of them logical (she resembles his mother) and some paradoxical; but at the first flimsy pretext he renounces her and goes to live in town (341ff.). Unfortunately, he finds no peace there. It remains for the itinerant Dr. Antelope, presently in town in his newly adopted profession as an evangelist, to explain why. The terms he uses are similar to those used by Monsieur de Milo in *Long Hunt*: "You are here," he says, "because you cannot go back, and cannot go on. . . . You have tried to go on. . . . You have also tried to escape without going on. . . . [Even] if you break away and wander over the earth you know that you will not escape. You did not escape . . . when you came west; you have not escaped by leaving the ranch; you will not escape

where you are going or whatever you do. There is no escape
from thoughts . . . except in the mind" (379f.).

Eventually, Ray returns to the ranch and begins a painful
reconciliation with Nancy. The reconciliation, of course, is
metaphoric; it is a reconciliation not only with Nancy, but with
the terms of life itself; and it is at best an uneasy peace founded
on irreducible anxiety. In a Naturalistic system, the most awe-
some predators are the phantoms that prey on man's imagination: "No one could read the system. On Bitter Creek the bears
were denning up and in the spring he'd hunt them and they
would hunt the weak calves and break up the houses of the
ants. The ants would pick the bones of the bear he killed.
Everything hunted and was hunted. But bears and ants knew
what it was that hunted them. Men didn't know." Against such
contingency and ambiguity, Ray finds a stoic resilience to be
the only possible defense: "So let the specks not grieve too hard
about their little lives, so lost in darkness under stars. . . . Let
[them] take what was bad with fortitude . . . and what was
good with gratefulness" (421).

Western scenes, motifs, and themes appeared importantly in
American literature throughout the nineteenth century,[29] but
the Western is a creation whose advent had to await the development of the range-cattle industry in the final third of the
century. Beginning in the early 1860's and developing in the
novels of Prentiss Ingraham, Sam Hall, William G. Patten, and
others, the cowboy and his environment emerged as well-defined
literary conventions by the end of the century.[30]

The novel that represents the culmination of these developments in the nineteenth century, and that is still often considered the archetypal Western or Western romance is Owen
Wister's *The Virginian* (1902). Wister frankly presents the
Virginian as "the last romantic figure upon our soil." The West
itself is romanticized, as well: "No lotus land ever cast its spell
upon man's heart than [*sic*] Wyoming had enchanted mine,"
the narrator says.[31] What little Realism graces the novel is
subservient to an overriding decorum. On one rare occasion the
Virginian enters into some "elemental talk of sex" (411), but
the narrator tells his "dear readers" that it "would be offence"
to repeat it. The faults of *The Virginian* as a novel are numerous; it is relatively barren thematically, characterization is thin
and uneven, action is episodic, and the slight plot arises from the

antagonisms of heroes and villains. The main business of the novel is the love affair between the Virginian and the New England schoolmarm Molly Stark Wood. Realizing that he loves above his station, the Virginian educates himself by reading Shakespeare and Dostoevsky, Browning and Jane Austen. He rides the range with Molly's cherished copy of Sir Walter Scott's *Kenilworth* in his pocket, and at night he practices his penmanship. Molly finally comes to the Virginian on "the sure feet of love's steed" (275), and their wedded bliss is "better than [their] dreams" (499).

The Virginian is not without merit,[32] but its faults are so fatally attractive that they reappear in Westerns with alarming frequency. *Bitter Creek* is Boyds' weakest novel partially because it shares some of those faults. They do not occur in great profusion, but (as in Frost's New Hampshire) there is one of each: one Indian war and one abducted woman, one company of galloping cavalry and one barroom brawl. Two things were in Boyd's favor when he began the novel, however. One was that he designed it partially as a historical novel, a form which, as he now understood it, tended naturally to produce a Realistic rather than a Romantic portrayal of the West. The other was that the Western novel itself had to a degree undergone transformation since *The Virginian*. Emerson Hough's *The Covered Wagon* (1922), Edna Ferber's *Cimarron* (1930), and Conrad Richter's *Sea of Grass* (1937), for instance suggested that there were significant themes as yet untouched by the Romantic Westerns. As a result, *Bitter Creek*, although far from a perfect novel, did help to raise the status of the Western novel, which had been and frequently still is, as James Folsom has asserted, either "enjoyed in silence," approached with condescension, or "absolved absolutely from even the possibility of merit."[33]

Boyd's historical research for *Bitter Creek* was somewhat more extensive than for *Long Hunt*. He worked from such sources as James Cox's *Historical and Biographical Record of the Cattle Industry* (1895), Katherine Coman's *Economic Beginnings of the Far West* (1912), P. E. Byrne's *Soldiers of the Plains* (1926); standard works on the West by Frederick Remington, Frank Dobie, and Douglas Branch; memoirs of William F. Cody and Emmett Dalton; and both state and national folklore and historical quarterlies. He took massive notes on the cattle- and sheep-herding industries, social history, technology, folklore, clothing, speech, prices and wages, and Indian life.[34] As a result, *Bitter Creek* is fundamentally accurate historically.

With *Long Hunt,* however, and even to a degree in *Marching On,* Boyd had begun moving away from the elaborately detailed re-creation of a historical period toward a concern for the basic outlines of the epoch and the qualities of a particular type of consciousness. So far as *Bitter Creek* was concerned, the movement was fortunate; for, as James Folsom has convincingly asserted, the Western novel "is not about . . . the facts of Western history in any specific historical sense." It is about "the meaning which underlies the superficial facts of history. . . . It celebrates not history but the themes of history. . . ."[35]

It so happens, however, that many of the significant themes of western history were for decades so imbedded in and identified with sterile literary convention that a virtual excavation is necessary to show that they occur in a given Western romance. (Folsom's ingenious explication of *The Virginian* is a case in point.) But as a result of developments in both the historical novel (stimulated to a great extent by Boyd's own early novels) and the Western novel, the Western can now remain essentially Realistic and historical, and therefore credible, and yet treat the human truths of the West which are its primary concern. One of those truths may even be the persistence of the Romantic imagination in those who find themselves drawn to the West. The novelist has the option of portraying the historically authentic Romance impulses of the cowboy through psychological Realism, for instance, rather than through sentimental manipulation of plot. The cowboy does not have to ride off into the sunset; it is probably more accurate historically, and certainly more truthful in human terms, to suggest his desire to do so.

It has long been recognized that the final truth of the West is the truth of myth.[36] *Bitter Creek* is concerned at one level with some of the most persistent myths of human experience: a man's hatred for his father and his attraction to his mother, the longing for knowledge which a return to primal innocence presumably offers, and the persistence of radical evil in human nature. More crucially, however, *Bitter Creek* involves other mythic themes that are, if not peculiar to, at least strikingly characteristic of, American experience: simultaneous affirmation of both materialistic and idealistic contexts of value, and a simultaneous worship of and contempt for women, who are both identified with and radically distinguished from the land itself. The dilemma of the protagonist of many Western novels, including *Bitter Creek*, arises from the "simultaneous affirmation of two contradictory and mutually exclusive points of view" and their corresponding sets of values.[37]

Finally, one feature of *Bitter Creek* that not only sets it apart from many Western novels but, at the same time, gives it a more profound mythic dimension, is its strong element of Naturalism, with the resulting ironic, almost bitter tone.[38] The answer Ray Talcott receives as he scans the heavens at the end of the novel is not exactly the "high cold star on a winter's night" of Stephen Crane's "The Open Boat," but it comes close. It is only slightly tempered by the paradoxical romantic cast of his personality, but that slight tempering is crucial. As Don D. Walker has so cogently argued,[39] such a tempering allows the metaphoric resolution of paradoxes unresolved in history, and unresolvable by either a strictly Naturalistic understanding of man, which denies him freedom, or by a strictly idealistic understanding, which spares him doom.

CHAPTER *5*

Synthesis: *Roll River*

B OYD'S fourth novel, *Roll River*, is a coherent work of art in
its own terms, a synthesis of the subjects, themes, motifs,
and techniques of his other work, and the most effective fusion
of the historical and Realistic novel of his career. *Roll River*
elaborates and reexamines the problem of the artist in a materialistic society which Boyd first examined in his stories. It deals
with the nature and significance of war and with the strengths
and limitations of the democratic and aristocratic sensibilities
which were basic concerns of *Drums* and *Marching On.* Like
Long Hunt, it explores the paradoxical relationship between
freedom and security. It questions the implications of resistance
to inevitable change, examined earlier in *Marching On* and
Long Hunt, and later in *Bitter Creek.* As in the first three novels,
history is the basis of the narrative—the detailed social, political,
and economic history of an era that was so important in *Drums*
and to a lesser extent in *Marching On,* and the history of a
state of consciousness that formed the center of *Marching On*
and *Long Hunt.*

Such a synthesis makes *Roll River* both historical and Realistic in the full sense of both terms. It is faithful not only to
the surface details of dress, speech, and manners of four generations during a turbulent half-century but also to the values
and habits of mind of each generation. The result is a literal
and psychological Realism that is valid not only for the evanescent particulars of given periods in history but for the basic
constants of human experience—man's rage for order and his
apprehension of chaos, his desire for stability and his knowledge of flux, his self-protective isolation and his need for communion. In *Roll River,* Boyd intended to employ "the true
realism of the heart of man," to probe "the deeper realities beyond our knowledge." Insofar as such a reality could ever be

109

given expression, he said, it was the only quality of fiction that interested him.[1]

The technical problems Boyd faced in *Roll River* were larger and more complex than any he had ever faced. *Drums* covers a period of less than ten years; and, although the detail called for in connection with the uncouth Captain Flood or the elegant Wylie Jones is diffierent from that demanded by Johnny Fraser, each character type is distinct, coherent, and relatively stable during the action of the novel. The problem was less complicated in *Marching On,* where the time was even shorter and the number of types reduced. In *Long Hunt,* achieving historical authenticity in setting was relatively simple for the obvious reason that forests and rivers have changed little since the eighteenth century; the problem of psychological realism was essentially to create two basic types of personality—the long hunter and the settler.

Fortunately, Boyd himself had lived through most of the history he was writing about in *Roll River.* "[My] aim was to give the spirit of a class in an American town of the period," he told Horace Clute. "I [stuck] close to the physical details of Harrisburg ... because there, more than any other town I knew, or could perhaps create, they were beautiful and simple and symbolic."[2] This is not to say that *Roll River* is an autobiographical novel; it is not. But to those who know Boyd's biography intimately, the parallels are numerous and obvious.[3]

Contrary to the general practice of novelists in the 1920's and 1930's, Boyd had almost completely avoided autobiography in his stories and in his first three novels. In this sense, then, *Roll River* represents a radical departure from his earlier practice. But the crucial question for autobiographical no less than for historical detail is what it *becomes* in the imaginative system of the novel. We wish to know finally not where the details come from but how they *function* in the novel.

Boyd's earliest plan for what became *Roll River* is suggested by an early sketch for a novel tentatively named "The Tower Builders." The novel was never written, but its outline is visible in *Roll River.* It was to involve three generations of one family, tracing through them three states of consciousness—an "age of [pagan] faith," an "age of religion," and an "age of science."[4] Brief character sketches indicate that two of the three generations were to be represented by Boyd's father and grandfather. By the early 1930's, however, Boyd's ideas about writing had changed; and the early plan was no longer as acceptable as it would have been during his apprenticeship, when he thought of writing as a "craft."

Craftsmanship might govern form, but life could be breathed into materials, whatever their origin, only by subjecting them to the catalytic influence of imagination. Grandfather Rand, modeled physically on Boyd's grandfather, is "spiritually re-created in another image"; Tommy Rand, who in a few respects is similar to Boyd himself, is actually a composite of many boys Boyd knew.[5] The characters are therefore historically authentic but not historically identifiable; the life they have in the novel is their own. While Boyd was writing, he told Maxwell Perkins that he could never guess how the characters would act until they started to move. As for the final creation itself, he said, it is not the product of a craftsman who exercises absolute control over his materials but "only a fragment of a Leviathan in whose maw I . . . wander blindly."[6]

Boyd began his fourth novel as early as 1931, but a series of operations delayed him repeatedly. "I have been fighting sinus trouble and a novel, all winter long," he wrote to Ben Dixon MacNeill in 1932, "until I can't tell which is producing which."[7] By 1934, the first book of the novel was finished. It was published serially as "The Dark Shore" in *Scribner's Magazine,*[8] running concurrently with Fitzgerald's *Tender Is the Night.* When the completed novel went on sale April 25, 1935, *Roll River* sold somewhat slowly, perhaps partially because it was competing with Thomas Wolfe's *Of Time and the River* (1935) and Santayana's *The Last Puritan* (1935), both of which were very popular. Reviews of Boyd's novel were in general quite good, many of them calling *Roll River* the best and most important of Boyd's novels. Of the reviews in the more prestigious periodicals only the one in the New York *Times* expressed reservations.[9] The most important review, by Bernard DeVoto in the *Saturday Review of Literature,* caused Boyd great anguish.[10]

In the process of praising *Roll River*, DeVoto gratuitously attacked Wolfe's *Of Time and the River* and impugned the honor of the Scribner publishing firm. *Roll River* was "filled with characters who are hammered out of the American experience . . . and who are directed and controlled by a superb technician,"

DeVoto said; but Wolfe's characters were "Mardi Gras gro-
tesques who suffer from compulsion neuroses and walk on
stilts." He wondered "if only an accident of the calendar led
Scribner's to hold *Roll River* til *Of Time and the River* was well
launched, or whether capital investment had something to do
with it." DeVoto's long-standing dislike for Wolfe's work clearly
distorted his critical judgment. Both Boyd and Wolfe found
the atack irrelevant and uncalled for,[11] but thy respected each
other and each other's work so much that it caused no ill feelings
between them.

Wolfe, who had met Boyd even before *Look Homeward, Angel*
(1929) was published, had been "tremendously impressed" by
him.[12] Boyd liked Wolfe's first novel and subsequently recom-
mended him for a Guggenheim fellowship.[13] Wolfe received his
Guggenheim early in 1930 and was delighted to come across
the Boyds in Paris that summer.[14] For the next eight years Wolfe
and Boyd visited regularly in New York and Southern Pines,[15]
and there is evidence that Wolfe not only admired Boyd personally but learned something about writing from him.

Although Boyd by this time viewed writing as more than the
"craft" he had called it during his apprenticeship, he was still
convinced that a Flaubertian craftsmanship was necessary for
a coherent novel. Like many others, including DeVoto, Boyd
found the lack of form a major weakness in Wolfe's books, and
he often talked with him about it.[16] "You are a swell guy even
if you do have decided theories of form," Wolfe told Boyd just
after *Look Homeward, Angel* was published. "It will be a proud
day in my life when you wring my hand and say, 'Son, the
style and structure of your last book makes Flaubert look like
an anarchist. . . .' "[17] When Boyd wrote later to praise "The Sun
and the Rain," Wolfe replied that "your letter gives me hope
that I may finally be learning something about my job."[18]

Boyd's friendship with Wolfe remained free of the misunder-
standings that eventually alienated Wolfe from so many of
his other friends. Consequently, Boyd was able to serve, though
unsuccessfully, as an intermediary when the break approached
between Wolfe and Maxwell Perkins.[19] Partially because Boyd
was always impressed by the sheer power of Wolfe's life and
writing,[20] and partially because they were both concerned with
"the buried life," although in different ways, it is no accident

that their books were published the same year with similar titles.

I Roll River *and the Buried Life*

For all his gratuitous attack on Wolfe's *Of Time and the River,* De Voto commented astutely on *Roll River.* It was, he said, "a novel made up of many novels which are fused so thoroughly that they are indistinguishable but which pile up significance many layers deep."[21] Formally, *Roll River* is two novels, "The Dark Shore" (Book I) and "Toward Morning" (Book II), but the significance of their multidimensional motifs and themes blends and reaches far beyond the lives of their respective protagonists, Clara (Rand) Rankin and her nephew Tommy Rand.

"The Dark Shore" is Clara's story. Born about 1870 into a prosperous and respectable family of "Midian," a central Pennsylvania industrial town. Clara Rand grows up in a society that is inflexibly committed to a rigid set of social, religious, and familial pieties. The freedom promised her in her marriage to Fitz-Greene Rankin proves to be illusory because neither he nor she is capable of responding to it. Fitz-Greene's suicide soon after their marriage is the paradoxically appropriate result of life based on values that are themselves moribund. Clara spends the next thirty years searching her own buried past, as well as that of her family, learning what Fitz's death means. His death becomes the organizing center in an otherwise disorganized stream of events symbolized by the river that flows between her house and the distant, dark shore on the other side.

"Toward Morning" is Tommy Rand's story, the details of which are counterpointed against Clara's story in "The Dark Shore." Born about twenty years later than Clara, and having the advantage of being male, he passes through his early life with far less inhibition and frustration than she did. Returning from college as a dutiful son to take a position in Rand & Company, he marries Julia Wilton, an attractive but conventional girl, and settles comfortably but unenthusiastically into the respectability of Midian. The war intervenes, however, and Tommy's whole view of his experience is changed by his service in France. He finds his old life so intolerably constricted and dull that he decides to leave his wife and family. A final conversation with Clara, however, reveals to him the related meanings of both their lives, and he decides that he must stay and face the life he has made for himself.

Clara's problem was to find a place for her spirit in a world from which spirit has been exorcised; her struggle was to be herself in a society where authentic selves were not permitted. Tommy's problem is to know the deepest truths about himself, most of which are represented by Clara. His struggle is to respond to those truths, to the actual reality of his life. His learning, softened and given depth by Clara's strength and vision, is a movement toward morning.

Roll River is marked by a greater technical complexity and dexterity than Boyd ever achieved elsewhere. Flashbacks, dream sequences, streams of consciousness—virtually all the devices of the psychological Realist—are used not only to integrate the stories of Clara and Tommy but also to encompass within them most of the history of four generations of the Rand family and fifty years of Midian society.

II *"The Dark Shore"*

"The Dark Shore" and "Toward Morning" are integrated at the beginning through a retrospective narrative frame. Tommy Rand, who is in the hospital in about the year 1930, is at the point of death from having been gassed during a rescue operation in a coal mine. During two days, he thinks back over his whole life and Clara's. The ironic tone of his recollections is set first by his minute observation of the hospital room, which is itself both a problem of understanding, and an example of the paradoxical effects of knowledge, particularly of a scientific variety. The "noiseless, odorless, dustless, scratchless," floor, Tommy notes, is "a triumph of negation," a metaphor for the uniform unreality of the hospital, and a fitting arena for the "highly trained automata of science" who move silently across it to perform their supposedly humane duties.[22]

The hospital quickly becomes a metaphor for the whole unknowable cosmos (5), and Tommy's confinement symbolizes man's inherently limited experience. The impressions he receives are of darkness, masked faces, muffled voices, inscrutable actions, and distant sounds. The only item in the microcosm that Tommy feels sharply is himself, at the center of "ever-widening circles"

(6). At that center, he takes up the tangled thread of life and begins to follow it (9). His act of exploration is a recovery of a past that seems as dark and inscrutable and as bound by fate as the room where he lies.

The earliest event Tommy recalls involves Clara, who has always seemed to him somehow free of the "meaningless web" of fate that trapped everyone else (13), a center of radiance and apparent immunity who caused his child's world, "filled with dreads, obscurities and frustrate longings, to blossom into splendor" (12). But the process of recollection is inherently a simplifying one; Tommy knows now what he has learned only near the end of his life—that Clara's freedom is limited and conditional and that her serenity is a result of years of struggle. "The Dark Shore" chronicles those years.

The deadly, uniform respectability of Midian is suggested by the monotonous fronts of the brownstone houses that face the river (33), but the suggestion is not confined to them alone. Clothing is no less rigid and is even more significant metaphorically. Clara, who watches her brother George (Tommy's father) in his stiff shirt, stand-up collar, and starched duck trousers, imagines that each bending of his knees must produce a "structural collapse" (49). Clothing in Midian is chosen solely for its presumed appropriateness to the sacred rituals of respectability —excursions on the river, coaching, picnics, dinners, and parties. At one point, in a supreme example of piety, condescension, and romantic hypocrisy, Clara's mother sits as chairman of the board of a home for wayward girls. When Clara enters the room, she is met only by the "armored bosoms" of the women and by "a sort of uneasy vacuum, extemporized by worldly wisdom in honor of her virginity" (93).

There are a few advantages to such a limited system, but Clara learns that "the price that one must pay for them is far too high: constant surveillance ... [and] the inevitable pressure to penetrate one's individual spirit ..." (81). Only hardy souls like Uncle Mun Worrall and Jeanne Balso, the dark maiden of the narrative, can bear the condescending indulgence accorded to the elect but unregenerate. Clara's impeccable social credentials preserve her from condescension, but her spirit is nevertheless violated. She is neither far enough from the center of power to avoid its influence, as Jeanne Balso does, nor eccentric and extroverted enough to render it invalid, as Worrall can.

Clara's room is a Midian in miniature. Over her bed is a picture of the Infant Samuel with his eyes "raised with saccharine piety to Heaven" (40); her bookcase is filled with bland treatises on the spiritual life and with effete juvenile novels (41). But Clara herself is alive both spiritually and physically. She stands before a mirror and thinks of slipping her nightgown to the floor, but she is reproached by a picture of her finishing-school classmates, "Tight-waisted and tight-haired, their hour-glass figures buttoned to the neck in black" (41). Solemnly, she descends to the breakfast room, with its grapes carved in rigid relief on all the furnitue, and the rigidly prescribed ritual of the meal (42).

The crucial ritual for Clara is her approaching marriage. Determined that she shall make a "distinguished marriage," her parents are disturbed by her choice of Fitz-Greene Rankin. Relatively unknown in Midian, except for his gay, unconventional behavior in courting Clara, Fitz is unwelcome until the Rands discover, by elaborate but covert inquiries, that he is of a wealthy Philadelphia family. They are then willing to tolerate both his extroverted behavior and his engagement to Clara. The wedding, of which Mrs. Rand takes charge like "the captain of a frigate clearing for action," is a grotesque, meaningless formality (108).

Fortunately, Fitz is exactly suited to Clara—not as she is presumed to be by her parents, but as she is. Unfortunately, however, the Midian milieu acts not only to prescribe people's behavior but also to render them incapable of acting on their own legitimate impulses even when they are ostensibly free to do so. The tragic consequences of this influence are foreshadowed in Clara's frantic attempt to communicate with her mother before the wedding. "[Will] I be all right?" she asks, "Will I know what to do?" Mrs. Rand assures her evasively that "Of course it will be all right," and she immediately begins to make a list of the wedding gifts (114).

Not surprisingly, Clara's sexual response to Fitz is less than adequate; and Fitz passes successively through stages of patient compassion, frustration, and finally alienation. Too late they discover that they are "caught in a labyrinth . . . not of their own design" (182). Paradoxically, Fitz's ignorance is only slightly less than Clara's. On a trip to Philadelphia he contracts

a venereal disease from a whore and is too ashamed and frightened to see a doctor until he at least believes it is too late.
Totally withdrawn from each other, he and Clara act out
hideous rituals of togetherness—Fitz, tormented by guilt and
anxiety; Clara, desperately trying both to understand what is
totally hidden from her and to avoid bitterness.

When Fitz commits suicide, he does it in a way that suggests the whole Romantic unreality that has destroyed him and
his life with Clara. After an evening of ice-skating on the river
in the moonlight—in a scene straight from Clara's *Hans Brinker*
book—Fitz skates intentionally toward a hole in the ice and
drowns. Paradoxically, the skating itself had been a quasi-
sexual act in which Clara and Fitz finally achieved the unity
denied them in intercourse itself (206ff.). But Midian can react
to such a tragedy only in stereotyped ways. Mrs. Rand, unable
to feel it or to communicate with Clara, begins to make lists
for the funeral.

The tragedy is laden with paradox. It might have been prevented but for the decorum exercised in deference to Clara's
supposed innocence and purity, qualities assumed to make her
a perfect wife for Fitz. Clara's failure itself is in one sense the
result of strength rather than weakness. From her youth, she
frequently thought of herself as a man simply because a pseudo-
masculine role was her only access to the identity categorically
denied to her and to all women. She had an enormous capacity
to love, but she had to become masculine in order to find freedom to love. The final paradox lies in Clara's response to the
frantic attempts to rescue Fitz. She sees that for once decorum
was shattered, and people responded humanely to the real and
urgent necessities of the situation.

Fitz's death is the final event in Clara's education, and at
length she learns four crucial truths from it. She learns first
that she cannot return to the stable past, represented by her
father, sitting "so still and vast" in the house on River Street
(16). He was the "great bear of her universe" (114) when she
lived at home, and her anticipation of marriage was qualified
by her reluctance to leave him (101). But, after Fitz's death,
Clara sees that her father's stillness was illusory; he has changed
and can no longer act as a refuge for her.

Indeed, Clara learns that stasis itself is an illusion. The "toy

castle" (132) where she lived with Fitz becomes after his
death a place of memories she at first refuses to leave (231).
But even the memories are evanescent, and the house soon
seems "no stronger to hold her than the world outside" (247).
There can be, she eventually discovers, no escape from destiny;
and destiny at bottom is change.[23] Her final lesson is that
destiny, whatever it involves, ultimately has to be faced alone.
The human condition *in extremis* is a condition of radical
isolation.[24]

III   *"Toward Morning"*

Tommy Rand grows up in a child's variety of Clara's archetypal isolation. His mother is merely a "disembodied presence,
a central abstraction of the cosmos" (267). His father is more
substantial, but in his cold sternness and piety, he is no more
comforting. He is the virtual embodiment of Midian society:
in the evening he reads the *Midian News,* the *Strenuous Life,*
and the *Sunday School Lesson Illustrator* (360). The veneer of
life in Midian is smooth, but violence lies beneath (269). For
Tommy, the violence is "the profound and irreparable tragedies
of ... [the] life within" (272) that are partially created and
sustained by the contradictory attitudes of his parents toward
their own lives and toward him. While he is still young, he
learns that they are "powerless to help and [know] him not at
all" (273), and he therefore takes refuge in the adventures Clara
devises and in his own fantasies.

The pressures to conform are so great, however, and are applied
so systematically that eventually every impulse Tommy ever
had to break through the crust to the real life beneath is stilled.
He returns to Midian from Yale to take his place in John Rand
& Company. An infatuation with the vivacious Jeanne Thompson (a counterpart of Jeanne Balso in "Dark Shore") is terminated by Tommy's marriage to Julia Wilton. Julia, delicately
pretty and totally respectable, is prudish, sanctimonious, moralistic, and frigid. Unfortunately, Tommy is prepared to recognize none of Julia's limitations for what they really are because
he lacks a frame of reference in which they could be rightly
judged. The war eventually provides a frame that is as unlike
Midian as possible.

Tommy's actual involvement in the war as an infantry officer in France is a well-defined but relatively brief episode. Its significance is fundamental, however; it reveals to him that the hollow abstract idealism of the war is identical to that which governed life in Midian, where the churches came to life for the first time during the war years, and when Dr. Alwine preached on "The Sword of the Lord and of Gideon" (385). There is "too much talk," Grandfather Rand says, "All nonsense, these preachers and orators and women" (390). Tommy, after his service in France, agrees. He also recognizes that the snobbishness of Midian is totally unjustified. The manhood he had assumed to be the special possession of the Rands and others in similar circumstances he now knows is randomly distributed among the men who made up his platoon—northerners, southerners, city boys and country boys, upper class and lower class. Likewise, he knows that depravity is not confined to the lower orders.

Tommy's renewed acquaintance with Jeanne Thompson, a nurse in an army hospital at Neuvilly during the war, produces the most important change in him. He slowly realizes that he was afraid of Jeanne's "warmth and vigor" when they were in Midian (466). Because an honest response to her threatened every stereotype on which his life was based, he chose Julia, who fulfilled them all. His discovery through Jeanne "that women . . . might profitably be regarded as human beings" (474) is radical in its simplicity.

The changes in Tommy are so profound that repatriation is impossible in any complete sense; Midian no longer exists for him. Even during the war he knew that his letters home had to pass "through not only vast space, but through . . . uncounted years of time"(433). The victory parade on Midian's River Street is totally ironic: "[On] both sides of him the faces made a wall; . . . proud, stupid faces of old men . . . fat women wallowing in emotion, and the faces of girls bobbing like painted egg-shells on a stream" (483f.). Implicitly, one of the painted faces is that of Julia, whom Tommy now recognizes not as a woman who shares Jeanne Thompson's humanity, but as "the symbol of his emasculate ideals" (475), as "a being strange and sexless, descended out of interstellar space, or if a woman, then a woman from some dim, frigid valley of the moon" (537).

Julia is the only feature of Midian that is unchanged by the war; she is one of the "women without passion" who are immune to change. Preserved by her coldness from suffering, loneliness, longing, and bewilderment—all of the "desolation of unrealized dreams in a world that [cannot] find its gaiety and splendor"—and armored with "the smooth completeness of her obtuse self-righteousness" (539), Julia knows no mercy. She badgers Tommy because the war did not inspire him to return with renewed vigor to the arid routine of his life in Midian (509), and she chides him for not reading any "books on the spiritual life" (536). Tommy, who envisions only his becoming "the American husband till death did them part," cannot tolerate such a future (540).

Tommy's escape from the "chrysalis whose vast complexity of tiny fibres" imprison him (541), seems surprisingly simple. It remains for Clara to tell him that it is a sham and that his freedom is illusory: "You must be merciless to yourself if you want peace," she tells him. He must bear his misery (547f.). When Tommy returns to Julia, he discovers that his new understanding of his own life and hers has freed him. Since spiritual freedom exists in a sphere unknown to Julia, it is not subject to her oppressive prying.[25]

Tommy's "separate peace" rests on a world view and on an understanding of human personality that are vastly different from those supplied him by Midian, and it represents not only the metaphoric completion of his own life but also the end of an era in the development of consciousness itself. The problem of Clara's generation was in one sense how to achieve freedom to act; for Tommy's, it has been how to recognize and act on the basis of freedom that already exists. As Tommy lies in his hospital bed at the end of the novel, he is visited by Clara and by his own son. Each of the three generations has the defects of its qualities: his son Tad is free in a way he himself never was, not only to act, but also to avoid radical disillusionment. But Tommy wonders "what new mistakes [Tad] would invent and bequeath to succeeding generations as the characteristic of [his] age" (600). To be meaningful, acts must have consequences; and if they have consequences, they are likely to restrict freedom in some way in the future.

The necessity for action is absolute, however, as it was for Johnny Fraser in *Drums,* for James Fraser in *Marching On,* for

Murfree Rinnard in *Long Hunt,* and for Ray Talcott in *Bitter Creek.* Tommy Rand's act—the one that finally causes his death —is his sacrificial attempt to help rescue men trapped by a cave-in in one of his coal mines. Explicitly, the attempt is prompted by his feeling of guilt for not having enforced safety regulations, but implicitly it represents his admission that his own bases for action in the past were wrong. He acted in response to dead conventions and not to the vital needs of the present—to profane economic "necessity" and not to the real and sacred imperatives of human life.

IV   Roll River *as a Novel of History*

Roll River is not a historical novel in the conventional sense of the term, nor even in the refined sense that *Drums, Marching On,* and *Long Hunt* are. For *Roll River,* Boyd did no research such as he had done for his earlier novels; except for the war, no recognizable historical events or persons are crucially involved. In "Dark Shore," every event occurs in the immediate experience of Clara Rand; in "Toward Morning," the action takes place between about 1900 and 1930—in what is literally the present. The few really historical events alluded to occur in a partially fictional history that is only sketchily developed. Tommy's great-grandfather General John Rand, we learn, "had emerged from the war of 1812 . . . less discredited than most" (19); but that is all we know about him. The whole history of the Rand family until Tommy's birth is sketched in a single paragraph.

Every generation and every decade from about 1870 to 1930, however, is authentically depicted. For the earlier years the texture of Realistic detail could perhaps be called "historical authenticity," but the distinction would be nominal. We finally observe that historical authenticity and Realistic detail merge to produce a single effect. From the brass doorknob, golden oak doors, marble mantel, and rosewood piano of Grandfather Rand's house in the 1890's, to the "brass territs and blinker monograms" of George Rand's horse-drawn carriage, to the mahogany enclosure, zinc lining, and brass spigots of the bathtub in Clara's house, to the sound of coffee in Tommy's electric percolator and the synthetic materials of his hospital room ("Guaranteed to remain devoid of interest through the ages"), Realistic detail is profuse and precise. Its presence establishes the texture of each period with remarkable authenticity, and its subtle but forceful modulation suggests metaphorically the irresistibly kinetic quality of history that is the novel's major theme. Moreover, the Realism is not confined to details of architecture, transportation, manners, and haberdashery. *Roll River* is more than a social novel; it is also to a considerable degree an economic novel, a war novel, a Freudian novel, and what now may be called a "novel of history."

Many of the social-novel aspects of *Roll River* have already been discussed in connection with the Rands. There are, however, more levels of society in Midian than the Rands represent. Jeanne Balso, and Jeanne Thompson and her father, all of whom are well defined, are part of an upper middle class. The middle class is filled out by the lawyer Mr. Riser, other employees of Rand & Company who are sketched in outline, and by such figures as Major Singletarry (from Tommy's infantry unit) and his gum-chewing wife Sally Mae. A lower middle class is represented in considerable detail by the Heisdicks, a German couple who live on Grandfather Rand's farm; Mr. Terwilliger, who tried to help rescue Fitz; and others. The lower class consists of the Negroes who function primarily as house servants for the Rands (Susan Tarr, Samuel, Levi, and others), the poor whites who live up the river in Billy Goat town, and the oppressed miners and their families in the villages surrounding the Rand coal mines.

All of these characters are drawn in considerable detail, and their living conditions and manners are clearly represented. With the possible exception of the Negroes, every class shows considerable diversity among its members.[26] Even the Negroes Susan Tarr and Levi achieve something of an individual identity, though, as always in Boyd's work, it is marginal. One weakness of *Roll River* is that real sympathy for the lower classes is confined almost wholly to the miners. Billy Goat town exists as an offense to polite society, but it is not used as an example of human degradation that deserves sympathy.

The economic aspects of class structure are rather fully explored in *Roll River*. Grandfather Rand manages the lucrative mining business with old-style financial integrity. "All bills, if correct," he says, "are paid on the day received, all deliveries are made on the date specified" (377). Rand's integrity is qualified by Social Darwinism, however, as it was for so many of his counterparts. The coal business is a constant struggle for survival, with the rewards going to those astute enough to "grasp the ways and means of getting sidings and coal-pocket sites out of city councils" (20), to control the business "from its source, the mines" (371), and to avoid labor problems. "I don't like labor," Rand says. ". . . You will always have trouble with labor in the end" (492f.). Tommy Rand is reared in the tradition (he must give a strict account of how he uses his fifty-cent allowance every week), but the war separates him from it and substitutes other values for economic ones.

Bernard DeVoto once said that *Roll River* contained "the best presentation of the A.E.F. that has yet been printed.[27] The remark may be exaggerated; but, if we exclude E. E. Cummings's *The Enormous Room* (1922) and Hemingway's *A Farewell to Arms* (1929) because they do not deal specifically with fighting units of the Allied Expeditionary Force, little World War I fiction published before 1935 (besides Dos Passos's *Three Soldiers*) remains of a high quality.[28] The war occupies most of ten chapters (375-488) of "Toward Morning," and its nature and meaning are central issues not only for Tommy Rand but for most other characters as well. Tommy's unit trudges across the "gray churned earth . . . bent forward and crouching down a little in the cave that had been hollowed out for them in the great bursting world of death" (423). Digging frantically in a gun emplacement with his mess-kit cover "while the shell-fire plowed the German corpses overhead," Tommy feels "no better than the meanest grub or worm, no more heroic, no less ignorant of what [is] going on in the world above." Recalling tales of "immaculate British officers [who] walked about under fire encouraging their men," he decides "It must have been some other war" (429f.). Julia's assumption that Tommy's having fought in a war for lofty ideals will forever be an inspiration to him is ludicrous at best (472); for Tommy knows only that the idealism was largely false and that his own life must now be based on the most concrete human values.

When Tommy returns to Rand & Company after the war, the "complex unreality" of the coal business becomes real for the first time when he sees the "broken land of desolate ridges," the "washed-out rutted street," and the rows of "seedy houses" of

the mining country. His attempt to help rescue miners trapped
by a cave-in not only reveals the changes in his values—and
therefore in the whole economic metaphor—but also completes
the fairly persistent Freudian themes of the novel.

Fitz-Greene's suicide in "The Dark Shore," coming immediately after a substitute sexual experience with Clara, is in one
sense a return to the womb (207ff.). For Tommy, Fitz's death
represents the death of his father; he has made Clara and Fitz
substitute for the vague abstractions that are his real parents
(267ff.), and they have made him their child. The act of rescu-
ing the trapped miners is for Tommy an attempt to reverse the
metaphoric process by which Fitz perished, as well as to atone
for the complex sins of his own family's past. The imagery is
appropriately anal. The drift mouth, a "black hole framed in
timbers" (504), leads down to a cool, dark subterrranean cor-
ridor to where the masked rescue workers, with "big, blankly
staring eye-pieces set in black rubber faces that ran down into
shaking snouts" (590), work to burrow through the rock-fall,
lifting "black, enormous slippery weight[s]" into the cars to
be moved out of the mine (591). As the imagery so clearly
shows, Tommy is trying to relieve the constriction of an entire
system. Interestingly enough, the rock-fall was caused by the
hoarding attitude of Rand's father and grandfather (the fore-
man, under orders to operate as cheaply as possible, uses insuffi-
cient safety apparatus), which is itself a major motif in the
novel and an obvious dimension of the anal metaphor.

Roll River is not basically a Freudian novel, any more than
it is basically a social, economic, war, or historical novel. But
Freudian themes are important. The statement is a complex one
and must be made in complex terms. One of the strengths of
the novel is that there is an excellent balance and integration
of the various sets of terms in which it operates. As Bernard
DeVoto noted, it is "what a good novel must be: a novel made
up of many novels which are fused so thoroughly that they are
indistinguishable but which pile up significance many layers
deep."[29] Running through every layer, uniting them, and giving
every theme a larger significance than it might have alone, is
a sense of history.

Roll River is, finally, a novel of history. The themes of every
"layer" are present in historical depth. The social-novel aspects

of *Roll River,* as has been indicated, are presented in detail for four generations whose values and actions differ markedly from one another. Economic motifs and themes change to parallel the changing attitudes, values, and actions of the generations. Tommy Rand, for instance, evaluates the mining operations in essentially moral and humane terms, as opposed to his father and grandfather to whom the mines hardly even exist as palpable realities. Tommy sees the mining industry as "a welter of waste and exploitation" (555) that sustains itself through feudal tyranny over the lives of the miners. The significance of the war also varies radically for the different generations. Sexual mores are also involved in a historical flux.

Even the meaning of history itself is an issue which displays historical flux, since the historical authenticity of each generation is established partially by showing its attitudes toward history. To Grandfather Rand, the past is part of a process leading to the present more or less in evolutionary terms; the process is neither subject to control nor open to value judgment. If he has a philosophy of history that can be defined, it is as we have noted, a Social Darwinist one. George Rand is a man for whom the past exists only as artifact; his consciousness is nearly ahistorical, and he therefore lives in a specious present. To Tommy Rand and Clara, the past and the present are one, as they must be for people of intense memory; and the present, though it may not deny the past, may by faith and will be transformed to produce a future more satisfying in human terms. Tommy's son Tad sees, in Robert Heilbroner's terms, the future as history—an infinitely receptive and infinitely malleable universe is open to the strivings of those who know how to manipulate its laws.[30] If, as Heilbroner suggests, such a conception of history is endemic in the American consciousness, what we see in *Roll River* is a subtle metamorphosis of the idea during four generations—and the particular strengths and weaknesses deriving from it.

CHAPTER *6*

The Free Company of Players: 1940-1941

ONE of the difficult questions facing American writers in the late 1930's was whether to become involved in the debate over the rise of totalitarianism in Europe and its implications for American society. Was one to become a propaganda tool of the state? If so, arguments and opportunities for doing so were numerous. Was one to stay out of the controversy altogether? If so, one's decision would seem to be sanctioned by attractive precedents. Was one to become *personally* involved, but try to keep his *art* free of ideological commitment? If so, he seemingly denied the integration of personality from which his work presumably derives validity. Was one to write on ideological themes, but try to keep his writing from becoming thesis-ridden and therefore unliterary? If so, the results of such attempts in the past would suggest that failure is rather more likely than success.

American writers responded to the issue in a variety of ways—from Ezra Pound to Archibald MacLeish, from Robert Lowell to Stephen Vincent Benét—depending partially on their personal conception of the general social function of literature. If a writer felt it had no such function, his decision was relatively simple. If he believed it either could or *should* have such a function, the decision was complicated by subtle shades of philosophical, ideological, and esthetic value. As we may observe in *Drums, Marching On,* and *Roll River,* as well as, to a lesser extent, in *Long Hunt* and *Bitter Creek,* James Boyd felt that the artist and society share certain vital concerns. Among them was the maintenance of the intellectual and spiritual freedom essential not only to the wholeness of a personality and of a society but also to the continued viability of the artist's role in society.

What disturbed Boyd in the late 1930's was that such affirma-

126

tions seemed to be lacking not only among the public but also among artists, most of whom seemed "lost in uncertainty." "What is vitiating our [writers'] life and work," he wrote to Sherwood Anderson early in 1937, "is not precisely lack of a program for saving mankind which we can undertake—But lack of faith that there is such a program anywhere or ever will be.... But now no one wants to win the world for anything & so would not understand a writer who wished to do it or see it done.... It's this spiritual vacuum that's given the chance to dictators to claim the attributes of godhead & concoct a pietistic chauvinism out of lassitude and despair & latent tribal frenzy...."[1]

By 1939, the sense of uncertainty among writers had somewhat abated. Tentative steps were being taken to try to fill the "spiritual vacuum," but most of them were ineffectual. In March, Paul Green, Marc Connelly, Elmer Rice, and a few other writers (Boyd was not among them) explored "plans for a series of radio plays on democracy," but nothing developed from the meeting.[2] The American Civil Liberties Union, of which Boyd was a member, also contemplated a series of radio plays but did not produce them.[3] In July, 1940, Boyd declined Maxwell Perkins's invitation to write a statement about democracy for a series to be syndicated by the National Educational Association; for Boyd considered the plan as neither positive nor comprehensive enough. To achieve the desired results, Boyd felt, statements should have to be broadly conceived and directed to the widest possible audience.

Although most previous attempts to inform the American public about the significance of the war had been in the form of counterattacks on enemy propaganda, Boyd insisted that "the best defense would be the positive restatement... of the principles on which our government rests."[4] By early October, plans had begun for a "series of nationwide [radio] broadcasts on ... basic civil rights to be given under the auspices of the Department of Justice."[5] Boyd summarized his plan as "a proposal to meet our dangers in the field of ideas, not defensively and not by professional propaganda, but by giving a chance for free expression to that group of Americans uniquely qualified to present our beliefs, not as abstractions, but as a living spectacle made actual to the mind by color, drama, and passion."[6]

There were to be thirteen thirty-minute radio plays by American writers, and they were to begin during the winter broadcast season of 1941. Final plans specified that broadcasts were not to "initiate a social program" but were to be aimed at "taking stock of our present assets"; that they were to be dramatic rather than didactic or expository; that both writers and actors were to volunteer their services; and that the Department of Justice was to exercise no control whatever over the broadcasts. Late in November, Boyd sent letters to artists he believed would join the Free Company of Players, as the group was to be called: Archibald MacLeish, Sinclair Lewis, Ernest Hemingway, Marc Connelly, John Steinbeck, Orson Welles, S. N. Behrman, Stephen Vincent Benét, Thornton Wilder, Eugene O'Neill, Louis Bromfield, George Kaufman, and George M. Cohan. Besides these, Elmer Rice, Robert Sherwood, and Maxwell Anderson had already joined.

Early replies indicated that sponsorship by the Department of Justice might be objectionable. Some writers feared that their scripts might be submitted to government censors. Repeatedly Boyd assured them that they could write as they wished.[7] Late in November, MacLeish and Connelly joined the Free Company. William Saroyan, who joined a few weeks later, immediately began writing a play. Within a matter of days, he sent Boyd *The People With Light Coming Out of Them,* based on a recent incident in which teachers had been intimidated by a war veterans' league.

Response from other writers to the idea of the Free Company broadcasts was mixed. Ernest Hemingway, who first declined the invitation, later agreed to write a play but never actually did so. His delays, refusals, and renewed acceptances continued until late April, 1941, just before the series ended.[8] Orson Welles volunteered to write on freedom of assembly, but he wanted to know first whether the broadcasts would be censored. Boyd wired back a categorical "No," and Welles joined the Free Company. Of the other writers to whom Boyd sent letters, only Sinclair Lewis refused to join. He liked the idea, but other work prevented his becoming involved. Eugene O'Neill wanted to join, but his health prevented it.[9] Steinbeck, who joined early in February, said he would have to wait two or three months to write. Before the series actually began, twelve writers had promised scripts, and several were in hand.

With Saroyan, Rice, and Sherwood, Boyd approached the Columbia Broadcasting System to ask them to donate broadcasting facilities for the plays. Executives of the company were "In principle ... responsive but dubious of the outcome," Boyd said later. "They spoke of an anonymous lady who had once promised a constellation of authors who had not materialized. We said that we were not an anonymous lady."[10] After brief negotiations, Columbia agreed to donate air time and coast-to-coast facilities, as well as production, direction, and music. Eighty-nine out of one hundred and twenty-nine affiliated stations agreed to carry the broadcasts, an uncommonly high coverage. To make it easier for actors to participate, Columbia arranged for most of the broadcasts to originate in Hollywood. Burgess Meredith went to California to recruit actors and actresses, and among the nearly fifty who eventually donated their services to Free Company productions were Franchot Tone, John Garfield, Charles Bickford, Elia Kazan, Canada Lee, Nancy Kelly, Claire Trevor, and Agnes Morehead.

By the end of the year, plans for the series were reasonably firm. The working committee for the Free Company consisted of Boyd as national chairman, Burgess Meredith as chairman of the actors' division, Robert Sherwood as chairman of the writers' division, W. B. Lewis of Columbia Broadcasting System as chairman of the radio division, and Leith Stevens, also of Columbia as chairman of the musicians' division. Plans had moved rapidly, despite several persistent problems, not the least of which was psychological depression among some of the members. "If only these great evils might pass and we might be together more," Boyd wrote Paul Green from New York, "and if not happy at least free to grieve over the ills that occur between man and man, and not the great juggernaut of nations. . . . I will hang on until . . . [we] have time to . . . have a drink and assume that the world is a little more as it should be, or even, God help us, a little more as it used to be."[11] Lack of press coverage also hampered the Free Company's efforts. New York newspapers virtually ignored the formation of the Free Company and its broadcasts, even though Boyd held several press conferences.[12] Coverage in news magazines was also sparse.

Boyd also received many letters, even before the first broadcasts, from people who either expressed reservations about the idea of the Free Company or who questioned the motives of all its members.[13] To each letter, he sent essentially the same reply: "Whatever our views on [the war], we unite in our faith in the American principles of government . . . and in those principles only."[14] A final problem that had to be settled was the Free Company's relationship to the Department of Justice. It had become increasingly clear that its sponsorship would seriously limit the impact of the programs and would imply a degree of control that, however slight, was unacceptable to the writers. Late in January, before the first program went on the air, Boyd decided not to accept sponsorship by the Department of Justice.

I *The Free Company Broadcasts*

At two o'clock on Sunday afternoon, February 23, 1941, the first play, William Saroyan's *The People With Light Coming Out of Them,* was broadcast.[15] Later plays were to concentrate on specific civil rights in a democracy, but Saroyan's was on a more general subject: the synthesis of various ethnic and national groups into a coherent society whose members have common values and aspirations. "I like it here," says the protagonist at the end, "because the best people from all over the world is growing here into the first real nation of the world— the American nation—the nation of *human* people—the people with light coming out of them" (22).

The theme of the play, that people's "casual everyday humanity" is "stronger than any other power in the world" (22), is overtly stated rather than implied by the simple action. Reviewers were quick to point out that Saroyan's play had little irony, dramatic complexity, or thematic subtlety. It did, however, have the lucidity, focus, compactness, and essential thematic integrity that Boyd desired. "Bill Saroyan's play was not liked by the reviewers," he told a friend, "but it was liked by the people, who are writing in great numbers."[16]

The March 2 broadcast was Marc Connelly's play on freedom of speech, *The Mole on Lincoln's Cheek.* It was based in part upon recent attacks by the American Legion upon the secondary-school social-science texts of Professor Harold Rugg. *The Mole on Lincoln's Cheek* was a plea for truthful acknowledgment of both the virtues and defects of the American system, and particularly for the freedom to discuss its limitations with impunity. "Academic freedom is the first liberty to die when dictators rule," said the announcer at the end of the play, "for dictators know the power of education" (52). The American Legion did not attack the play, but others, such as Augustin G. Rudd, chairman of the New York chapter of the Guardians of American Education, Inc., objected strenuously to Professor Rugg's texts, to the play, and to Connelly personally.[17]

The general public continued to receive the broadcasts enthusiastically. On March 9, Robert Sherwood's *An American Crusader*, based on the life of the martyred Abolitionist newspaper editor Elijah Parish Lovejoy, was presented. Dramatically and thematically it was more unified and therefore more powerful than either Saroyan's or Connelly's; but like them, it was frankly didactic, and its characters were, therefore, one-dimensional.

On March 16, Boyd's *One More Free Man* was broadcast as the fourth play of the series.[18] It is about a young man who sacrifices himself in the cause of organized labor during the early years of the twentieth century. The play, made up of the prophetic visions of a pioneer woman, was more complex structurally than any of the earlier ones. "I am a daughter of the pioneers . . . who worked, took chances and winning, losing, made this land," the woman says. "Out of my nameless body, let there come a man who speaks the truth he knows, one more free man to make his country great" (114). The thematic complexity of the play is increased through several levels of allusion—an element absent from earlier Free Company plays. The birth of John Cross is explicitly analogous to the birth of Christ, and his mother is reminiscent of the pioneer woman in Hart Crane's *The Bridge*.

The March 23 broadcast was Stephen Vincent Benét's *Freedom's a Hard-Bought Thing*, a dramatization of his 1940 O. Henry Memorial Prize short story about a runaway slave.[19] The play is identical to the story in subject, theme, and tone. It differs from it only in that it is thinner in narrative texture (the plantation milieu is barely outlined), that the scenes are telescoped, and that the relationship between them is simplified both dramatically and thematically. The most important difference between Benét's play and earlier ones in the series is that, although its theme is just as insistent, it arises more through

characterization and action than through overt statement. The
narrator is used merely to connect the scenes, not to provide
interpretative comment on the action.

Orson Welles's *His Honor the Mayor*, which continued the
series on April 6,[20] is essentially a dramatization of Voltaire's
famous statement: "I disapprove of what you say but I will
defend to the death your right to say it" (174). It openly casti-
gates racists, anti-Semites, Fascists, and jingoists. Although the
tone is well balanced, the theme is subtle enough to allow mis-
interpretation by anyone unaccustomed to subtlety or by anyone who wished for some reason to misunderstand. Of both
groups there proved to be no dearth.

II   *Attack from the Right*

The American Legion had been irritated by Connelly's *The
Mole on Lincoln's Cheek*, but it had not responded directly
to it. Unfortunately, *His Honor the Mayor* refers to the American
Legion by name (157). Moreover, the cast of *His Honor* was
drawn from Welles's Mercury Theater, and most of the actors
were the same people who had starred in Welles's motion picture *Citizen Kane*, which had its New York premier just before
His Honor was broadcast. William Randolph Hearst, aged mag-
nate of the Hearst newspaper chain, had for months been fighting Welles over *Citizen Kane*.[21] Welles's Free Company play
was also broadcast just as the *American Legion Magazine* concluded its campaign against Professor Rugg's textbooks (the
incident treated in Connelly's play),[22] and just before the
American Legion national convention opened in Indianapolis.
Such a fortuitous conjunction of circumstances focused the ire
of both Hearst and the legion directly on the Free Company.

The Hearst attack began on April 21 when the Los Angeles
Examiner printed (without permission) a congratulatory letter
that Francis Biddle had written to Burgess Meredith after the
first Free Company broadcast.[23] The *Examiner* accompanied the
letter with vague speculations about subversive government
control of broadcasting, un-Americanism, and the like. The
story, which moved rapidly across the country in the Hearst
papers, became increasingly exaggerated until it made head-
lines in the New York *Journal-American*. The Hearst animus
was directed primarily against Welles, but it was sufficiently

loose in its condemnation—referring to Welles as a "leading force" in the Free Company, and finally to "Mr. Welles' Free Company"—to engage those who nourished tenuously related grievances.

Augustin G. Rudd of the Guardians of American Education renewed his attack on what he considered to be Connelly's insidious and subversive *The Mole on Lincoln's Cheek*. Local American Legion posts, other veterans' organizations, and the California Sons of the American Revolution found sinister statements in previous plays, as well as in three that had been broadcast since Welles's. Homer L. Chaillaux, chairman of the American Legion's National Americanism Commission, found the plays "cleverly designed to poison the minds of young Americans." An unnamed spokesman for a legion post in Brooklyn, reported *Time*, observed that "The name itself, 'The Free Company,' sounds suspiciously Communistic."[24]

As soon as Boyd received word of the Hearst-Legion coalition against the Free Company, he wired Milo J. Warner, the American Legion's national commander, for an explanation. Warner declined to reply to the substance of Boyd's inquiry, but he indicated that the matter would be considered by the legion's Americanism Commission in its session April 29, and he also invited a representative to appear before this commission to defend the Free Company's activities.[25]

Incensed by Warner's response, Boyd replied that "Although this [Free Company] office was established January 27th ... no protest has ever been received from any unit of the American Legion, and no [Legion] representative ... has ever made contact with us to ascertain ... whether the allegations being made were accurate." To the legion's invitation to a hearing, he responded: "Our office is here [in New York], and doing business; we welcome an investigation by the authorized representatives of any bona fide group; to any such persons our files are open for examination...."[26]

Ignoring again the substance of the issue, the legion's National Executive Committee adopted on May 2 a resolution calling the Free Company broadcasts "not conducive to the teaching of sound Americanism" and instructing the Americanism Commission to take "all necessary steps" to prevent additional broadcasts.[27] Fortunately, the Hearst-Legion attack was virtually ignored by news media outside the Hearst chain. The attack had, moreover, a favorable side effect: within two weeks, the Free Company's audience more than doubled, and mail became heavier and more enthusiastic than it had ever been.

The Free Company broadcasts continued on April 13 with Paul Green's *A Start in Life*, a dramatization of his earlier story, "A Fine Wagon."[28] Avoiding didactism, it treats subtly and profoundly the hopeless plight of the Negro in America—his spiritual blindness, his dogged plodding in the ruts of custom that lead nowhere, his piteous subservience to "white folks," and his desire for the self-respect that is denied him both from society and from within himself. The "message" of Green's play is less apparent than that of some of the earlier Free Company plays, but its themes are larger, more fundamental, and more complex.

The final three Free Company plays (April 20-May 4) brought to a focus the issue of propaganda. Boyd had intended from the beginning that the messages of the plays should be communicated through "the method of the Bible parable, of Aesop's fables"[29]—methods which imply that a lesson or moral may be explicitly drawn. For the better plays, conclusions were supplied primarily by the announcer (sometimes Boyd himself) at the end of the broadcast and were, therefore, separate from the plays. In some cases, they amounted only to a pertinent quotation from Lincoln, John Adams, or Voltaire; but sometimes they were more explicit (cf. p. 52). For the weaker plays, such commentary was gratuitous since the characters are mere spokesmen of the message.

In Archibald MacLeish's blank-verse *The States Talking*, broadcast on April 20, the "characters" are the states themselves ("There's talk on the east wind, says Illinois"), and their message is reiterated almost hypnotically: the "mixed race" of American men will not allow itself to be threatened by the rising Aryan tide. The "great strong laughing voice of America," said the announcer at the end, is "easy-going, but confident and sometimes even dangerous for those who will not understand" (236). This statement was the closest that any Free Company broadcast ever came to advocating war.

Maxwell Anderson's *The Miracle of the Danube*, broadcast April 27, provided a counterbalance for the pro-American stridency of *The States Talking* by telling the story of a conscience-tortured German army officer who performs acts of mercy that finally bring about his own humiliation and death. Explicitly, the play is about religious toleration (the officer helps prisoners to escape the Nazis); but at a deeper level it affirms man's unquenchable religious spirit and the necessity for freedom to exercise it.

The Free Company series closed on May 4 with Sherwood Anderson's *Above Suspicion*.[30] Its general theme was freedom from police persecution. The situation is simple: a refugee from Germany visits his American cousins and is introduced to the unaccustomed freedom of life in an open society. Despite its explicit condemnation of the German police state, the play is not anti-German. The family Fritz visits are of German extraction (they speak with great fondness of "the old country"), and the play ends with a Lutheran choir singing (in German) "Ein feste Burg."

In terms of Boyd's original intentions for the Free Company, the broadcasts could only be considered successful. The eleven plays had a weekly radio audience of nearly five million people, up to that time probably the largest ever to hear a series of serious broadcasts. The Free Company had also distributed thousands of copies of the individual plays, and it had given countless permissions for them to be performed in local communities. Carl J. Friedrich called the broadcasts "marvels of genuine pro-democratic poetry, broadly gauged in their conception of freedom, and hence suitable for reproduction in every home and school room in the land."[31] Moreover, thousands of recordings of the broadcasts were distributed for use in schools and hospitals.

During the summer Boyd made tentative plans to continue the Free Company broadcasts in the fall on an even larger scale.[32] MacLeish had submitted his *The Fall of the City* late in May for the new series,[33] and Boyd was planning to engage additional writers (Lillian Hellman, Elmer Rice, John Steinbeck, Carl Sandburg, Irwin Shaw, and others); but the broadcasts were not continued. Why they were not is not clear. Francis Biddle says in his autobiography that the Columbia Broadcasting System, "buckling down under the attack of the Hearst press," announced that the series would not continue,[34] but his statement has thus far not been corroborated. The Free Company series ended May 4, 1941.[35]

III *The Free Company in Retrospect*

Some intriguing questions about the Free Company remain: Did the writers who participated fulfill their proper responsibility as artists, or betray it? Were the plays art, or propaganda, or both? Was the net result of the venture desirable or undesirable, and in what terms and for whom?

It is important to realize first that the Free Company did not occur as an isolated incident. Nor did it, even as an idea, come into being quickly. The argument over the artist's proper role in a society and his relationship to the ideological debates of a society in turmoil had intensified during the mid- and late 1930's, and, early in 1940, Archibald MacLeish had evoked violent response by declaring that American writers and scholars were acting irresponsibly in the face of the Nazi threat to "the common inherited culture of the West."[36] The artificially separated functions of writer and scholar had to be joined again, he said, in "the man of letters" who would be "responsible in everything that touched the mind," who would employ his mind and his pen "for the sake of decent living in his time."

Response to MacLeish ranged from blanket endorsement to categorical rejection. Van Wyck Brooks called the essay "a splendidly moving statement that may turn the tide of American literature." John Gould Fletcher said it was "merely another attempt . . . to lower the values of knowledge before the values of action."[37] Scholars such as Perry Miller, Willard Thorpe, and Kenneth Murdock who responded to MacLeish generally admitted the symptoms he pointed out; but some disagreed about their causes and proper remedies.[38]

Poets and novelists, who generally rejected MacLeish's charge, usually followed the line of argument suggested by John Gould Fletcher. Going even further than Fletcher, James T. Farrell said that "Literature, by its very nature, cannot, in and of itself, solve social and political problems."[39] The final result of the "politicization of literature" that MacLeish and Brooks advocated, Farrell concluded, would be a "state literature" produced by writers who are told "what to do, what to write . . . and what to think." A more compelling argument came from Allen Tate, who said the poet's first responsibility is to the reality of life itself. If the writer responds to that intensely, what he writes will be vital; and it *may* then have an *indirect* influence upon action.[40]

To unravel the ironies, paradoxes, and outright contradictions of the arguments advanced by writers in response to MacLeish would be impossible here; for too many individual careers, sets of values, and points of view are involved. The argument may indeed be irresolvable in any final sense, but perhaps the issues may be named and the specific consequences for a particular event assessed.

We may observe at the outset that there were precedents for the Free Company venture. Harold Clurman, founder of the Group Theatre (1931-41), suggests that it was precisely to achieve a sense of the theater in direct relation to society that this group was formed. Before 1931, he said, most theater people were concerned only with strictly literary questions; they never dreamed of saying "This is our world, and it bodes no good."[41] But the avowed purpose of the Group was to "lead to the creation of a tradition of common values, an active consciousness of a common way of looking at and dealing with life."[42] Three of the Free Company's writers—Paul Green, Maxwell Anderson, and William Saroyan—also wrote plays for the Group Theatre; and others were in various ways involved in the political and ideological activism of the 1930's, both in the theater (which was itself more politically and socially conscious then than it has been since[43]) and outside it.

It is interesting to note that the response of almost all of the writers Boyd approached was immediate and positive. Those who refused did so for practical reasons only. The literary quality of the plays was not high, as has already been pointed out; but it is difficult to see how the failings can be attributed solely to the conception of the series. At least three of the plays (Paul Green's, Benét's, and Walter Clark's) were dramatizations of novels or stories written previously; and there was little loss of literary quality in the transformation.

No easy generalizations can be made, on the basis of the Free Company episode, about what happens to literature when it becomes wedded to an ideology, but it is impossible to regard the venture as one in which art came under the direct control of the state and was thereby debased. The name of the Free Company was chosen carefully; from the beginning, its letterhead carried Whitman's statement: "I say there can be no salvation for these states... without free tongues, and ears willing to hear the tongues." The Free Company plays were hardly Whitmanian in subtlety or power, but they were indeed so in spirit and motivation; it would be difficult indeed to conclude that the writers who participated did so at the cost of their responsibility as artists.

The "art or propaganda" question is also difficult to resolve. The Free Company plays were definitely not propaganda in any clear sense; they were not the cynical expressions of writers paid or forced to concoct a defense or justification for a narrow and pernicious political program or ideology. On the other hand, the plays were frankly didactic, and as such they lacked the range, depth, and subtlety one justifiably expects in good art.

Paradoxically, although the themes of the Free Company plays may in retrospect seem too insistent, the diversity of people's responses to them at the time suggests that they were taken to be less clearly didactic than they now appear. The same plays were accused by different listeners of being both isolationist and interventionist, pro-American and anti-American, radical and reactionary.[44] Nevertheless, under the *actual* circumstances and given the *actual* alternatives available to American writers in the early months of 1941, the goal of the Free Company was a worthy one, and its accomplishments were far more useful than detrimental.

CHAPTER 7

Conclusion

MY intention has not been to maintain that James Boyd was a great modern writer who has been mysteriously neglected. But he was a good writer, and his work deserves, because of both its intrinsic value and its influence, more careful attention than it has received. The range of Boyd's accomplishment was broad—five novels, two dozen short stories and about as many poems and essays, as well as several short plays. His literary career was also important outside his own writing. The Free Company of Players (1940-41), which he organized and directed, involved more than a score of major American writers; the Southern Pines *Pilot*, which he rebuilt and edited for four years before his death, remains as testimony to his conviction that a writer has an immediate responsibility for the quality of life about him.

Stylistically, Boyd's writing is controlled and carefully polished. At its best, his style is distinguished by a lucidity and grace that are poetic. Its weakness lies in a tendency to overwrite—to pile up images, to explain a metaphor, to rely from time to time on worn-out rhetorical formulas. Structurally and formally, the novels reveal Boyd's commitment to an esthetic that included craftsmanship as well as inspiration. Minor weaknesses of the novels are their relatively infrequent but annoying reliance upon coincidence in plot and action, and a tendency to equivocation in theme. But most of these problems seem minute in comparison with the merits of the novels in which they occur.

Boyd's subjects show considerable variety—the American Revolution in North Carolina; the Civil War; the opening of the trans-Appalachian frontier; the turn of the century in Harrisburg, Pennsylvania; and the last days of the range-cattle indus-

try in Wyoming. Fundamentally, however, he was concerned
throughout his career with one complex subject: the physical,
emotional, intellectual, and spiritual crises that attend the tran-
sition from one state of society to another—from colony to nation
in *Drums*, from feudal aristocracy to democracy in *Marching On*,
from wilderness and frontier to village and town in *Long Hunt*
and *Bitter Creek*, and from the Mauve Decade through the war
to the 1920's and 1930's in *Roll River*.

These transitions are depicted realistically in social, political,
and economic terms; but they are also mirrored metaphorically
in the consciousness of the protagonists. Most of Boyd's persistent themes arise through this mirroring: the desire for freedom and the need for security, the longing for stability and the
necessity of change, the persistence of the past in the social
order and in patterns of consciousness, and the quest to know
and act upon ideal and humane values in a universe which,
insofar as it is knowable, seems to operate on a rigid set of
Naturalistic laws.

James Boyd's reputation will rest finally on his novels, in
which these themes inform not only individual experience but
also the larger movements of history. If it is true, as is now
generally agreed, that the twentieth century has witnessed a
transformation and consequent revitalization of the historical
novel, James Boyd had a major role in the process. It is no longer
possible to say, as Hervey Allen did as recently as two decades
ago, that the historical novel is "a kind of mule-like animal be-
gotten by the ass of fiction on the brood-mare of fact, and hence,
a sterile monster."[1] Boyd and others have demonstrated that
the intentions of the Realist and the historical novelist are
complementary—not antagonistic—and that a historical novel
need be neither sterile nor a monster. A close reading of Boyd's
novels still suggests, as it did to Bernard DeVoto nearly thirty
years ago, that Boyd "so altered the *genre* that, largely as a
result of his work, it has become possible to discuss historical
fiction, simply as fiction, not as a special department of fiction."[2]

To understand the relationship in Boyd's novels between what
is normally considered as Realism and what has conventionally
been called "historical authenticity" (the only virtue commonly
accorded to even the best historical novels), we must understand that what the Realist is finally interested in is not the inert

(though accurate) detail of life in the present but in what might be called its spiritual ambiance—and that precisely the same thing is true of the historical novelist. No amount of tediously documented historical authenticity will give vitality to a novel unless the spiritual ambience of the period is a major aspect of that authenticity.

From *Drums* through *Long Hunt* to *Roll River* we observe a subtle shift in emphasis: the details of the social, political, and economic aspects of life in the period treated are attenuated as major preoccupations of the novel (although they remain to establish fully the texture of historical Realism in the conventional sense); and they are replaced by a concern for the emotional, intellectual, and spiritual realities of the era. The strength of Boyd's novels lies largely in their having captured this spiritual ambience and in his having made it the very center of concern.

We finally understand that even what seems to be equivocation in theme or point of view in the novels arises partially out of an attempt to establish a profound sympathy with the spiritual ironies, paradoxes, and crises of a remote age. Boyd's consciousness was finally in every respect a mediatory one. He attempted, both in his own experience and that of periods about which he wrote, not so much to level judgment as to understand, not so much to take a stance as to find legitimate grounds for sympathy. His mediation of those ironies and paradoxes arose not from weakness but from a profound awareness that experience *is* paradoxical and that a peace with it on any other terms is false.

"Wandering lost upon the mountains *of our choice*," says one of Auden's sonnets, "Again and again we sigh for an ancient South...." Like Auden, Boyd knew that paradoxically "We live in freedom by necessity,/ A mountain people dwelling among mountains." When he wrote for his newspaper in 1943— six months before his death—a short piece on the meaning of the American experience that had been so near the center of his writing for twenty-five years, he employed precisely Auden's metaphor and the paradoxes attached to it. We are at heart, he said, "mountaineers who have been raised in the high air of freedom.... Our mountains are rough and the life here often arduous and tumultuous, but few of those who have tasted our

Notes and References

Preface

1. Stanley J. Kunitz, ed., *Living Authors* (New York, 1931), p. 52.
2. "James Boyd," *Saturday Review of Literature*, XII (June 29, 1935), 10.
3. See for instance N. B. Fagin, ed., *America Through the Short Story* (Boston, 1937), p. 479; J. T. Frederick, comp., *Present-day Stories* (New York, 1941), p. 32; Richard G. Walser, ed., *North Carolina in the Short Story* (Chapel Hill, 1948), p. 159; and *North Carolina Authors: A Selective Handbook* (Chapel Hill, 1952), p. 9.
4. Letter to Paul Green, March 21, 1935; Southern Historical Collection, University of North Carolina; hereafter referred to as MSS—North Carolina. All quotations from collection used by permission.
5. Josephine K. Piercy, ed., *Modern Writers at Work* (New York, 1930), p. 911.
6. Boyd to Anderson, April 20, 1939; MSS—North Carolina.
7. Boyd to Anderson, May 24, 1939; MSS—North Carolina.
8. This is true of, for instance, Arthur H. Quinn's *American Fiction* (New York, 1936); Alfred Kazin's *On Native Grounds* (New York, 1942); the final "new directions" chapter of Alexander Cowie's *The Rise of the American Novel* (New York, 1951); and Frederick J. Hoffman's *The Modern Novel in America, 1900-1950* (Chicago, 1951).
9. Bernard DeVoto, "Escape to the West," *Saturday Review of Literature*, XIX (March 18, 1939), p. 6. Cf. Carl Van Doren's comment on *Bitter Creek* (whose title he gives incorrectly as *Bitter River*) in *The American Novel 1789-1939* (rev. ed.; New York, 1940), p. 362.
10. See for instance Edward Wagenknecht, *Cavalcade of the American Novel* (New York, 1952), p. 438.
11. See for instance Ernest E. Leisy, *The American Historical Novel* (Norman, Okla., 1950), and A. T. Dickinson, Jr., *American Historical Fiction* (New York, 1958). A notable exception is Robert A. Lively's *Fiction Fights the Civil War* (Chapel Hill, 1957), which treats Boyd's *Marching On* in some detail.
12. Bernard DeVoto, "A Novel Hammered Out of Experience," *Saturday Review of Literature*, XI (April, 1935), 645.

Chapter One

1. For various biographical details I am indebted to John W. Jordan, *Encyclopedia of Pennsylvania Biography* (21 vols.; New York, 1914), I, 60-62, and III, 1069n. Adam Boyd, a distant ancestor and editor of the Cape Fear *Mercury* prior to the revolution, has often been called Boyd's "great-great-grandfather," but it can be established that Adam Boyd died childless in Mississippi shortly after 1800. See David E. Whisnant, "James Boyd, 1888-1944: A Literary Biography" (unpublished dissertation, Duke University, 1965), pp. 303ff.

2. William H. Egle, *Centenary Memorial of the ... Founding of the City of Harrisburg* (Harrisburg, 1886), p. 125.

3. *Ibid.*, pp. 217f.

4. William H. Egle, *History of the Counties of Dauphin and Lebanon ... in Pennsylvania* (2 vols. in one; Philadelphia, 1883), pp. 356ff.

5. Letter to Horace Clute, July 10, 1935; MSS—North Carolina.

6. *National Cyclopaedia of American Biography*, XXVI, 421.

7. Manuscript fragment in the James Boyd papers at Princeton University. Hereafter referred to as Boyd Collection—Princeton. Quotations used by permission.

8. Undated letter [1902?] to his mother; MSS—North Carolina.

9. Letter of October 23, 1904; MSS—North Carolina.

10. Undated letter [1904?]; MSS—North Carolina. Mrs. Boyd was an active laywoman who became in later years a popular lecturer at Bible conferences throughout the East. She was the author of several study books on the Bible, and for several years she taught a Bible class of two hundred men at Pine Street Presbyterian Church.

11. Hill School *Record* (June, 1906), pp. 231f. Boyd frequently published articles, poems, and stories in the *Record* between 1904 and 1906: "Smith's Funeral" (story), May, 1904, p. 147; eight articles and four poems in the volume for 1904-5; and his prize story and class poem in the volume for 1905-6. Prior to 1904, he had contributed numerous drawings to school publications. For this information I am grateful to Mr. Paul Chancellor, librarian of the Hill School.

12. *Record* (June, 1906), p. 244.

13. Letter of February 17, 1908; MSS—North Carolina.

14. E. V. Lucas, ed., *The Gentlest Art* (4th ed.; London, 1908), p. 15.

15. *Ibid.*, pp. 15f.

16. Struthers Burt, "James Boyd, '10," *Princeton University Library Chronicle*, VI (February, 1945), 56.

17. Manuscript in Boyd Collection—Princeton. Quoted by permission. Boyd never dated manuscripts; the dating here is conjectural.

18. March 19, 1909; MSS—North Carolina.

19. James Boyd, *Eighteen Poems* (New York, 1944), p. 14. In a few rare copies of the volume, a different sonnet appears on p. 14. After publication the poem was discovered to belong to Marya Mannes of the *New Yorker*, who had sent it to Boyd for criticism. *Eighteen Poems* was published posthumously, and this poem was thought to have been Boyd's. When the mistake was discovered, a new page was inserted. A few editorial emendations were made when "Commencement—1910" was published, but it stands essentially as Boyd left it.

20. For information concerning Boyd's years at Princeton and Cambridge I am indebted to his classmates George Jones, Marion S. Wyeth, and Frederick Osborn.

21. Letter of October 9, 1910; MSS—North Carolina.

22. *Ibid.*

23. Letters of October 17 and 25, 1910; MSS—North Carolina.

24. From an unpublished sketch, "The Horse Guns," Boyd Collection—Princeton. Some information on Boyd's participation in the Corps is from an article of unknown date, "Military Instruction at Cambridge University," that he wrote for the *Princeton Alumni Weekly*. Copy in the possession of Jackson Boyd.

25. Letter of October 21, 1910; MSS—North Carolina.

26. Letters of January 18 through March 17, 1911; MSS—North Carolina.

27. See James Boyd, "American Hunting and English Standards," *Cavalry Journal,* XXI (1931), 117-24.

28. James Boyd, "Introduction," *Hunting Sketches,* by Anthony Trollope (New York, 1933), pp. xiv-xvi.

29. Cf. letters of February 14, March 17, and April [15?], 1911; January 2, 21, 22, 1912; MSS—North Carolina.

30. Cf. letters of January 15, 22, March 22, and April 11, 1912; MSS—North Carolina.

31. Cf. letters of April 11, 15, 18, 1912; MSS—North Carolina.

32. James Boyd, "University Life Here and Abroad," Harrisburg *Telegraph,* November 8, 1912, p. 7. Copy supplied by the Pennsylvania State Library.

33. Letters of October 18 and 24, 1913; MSS—North Carolina.

34. Letter of May 20, 1916; MSS—North Carolina. Copy supplied by Charles Norman.

35. Letter of May 1, 1915; MSS—North Carolina.

36. Letter of December 19, 1916; MSS—North Carolina. Copy supplied by Charles Norman.

37. Letter of December 19, 1916.

38. All quotations from letters of August 3 and 5, 1914; MSS—North Carolina. There is also a suggestion of chauvinism and anti-Semitism in the letter of August 3.

39. For many of the details regarding the Ambulance Service in the war I am indebted to *The Medical Department of the U. S. Army in the World War* (15 vols.; Washington, 1921-29), VII and VIII, *passim.* Information on the ambulance service not otherwise attributed is from this source.

40. For a reminiscence of Camp Crane and the war by a member of Boyd's unit see Julian R. Meade, "James Boyd," *Saturday Review of Literature,* XII (June 29, 1935), 10f.

41. Quoted by Struthers Burt, "James Boyd, '10," *Princeton Alumni Weekly,* XXXVI (November 22, 1935), 195.

42. Letter of November 25, 1918; MSS—North Carolina. Censorship prevented sending information on the movement of troops until after the Armistice.

43. *Ibid.*

44. Based on *ibid.*

45. "Humoresque," *Scribner's Magazine,* LXXXIII (April, 1928), 449. Subsequent quotations are from this source.

46. Letter of November 25, 1918; MSS—North Carolina.

47. *Ibid.*

48. Letter of January 3, 1919; MSS—North Carolina.

49. For Struthers Burt's account of Boyd's coming to see him to show him poems and stories he had written during the war, see *Princeton University Library Chronicle,* VI (February, 1945), 57. Several manuscript poems are in MSS—North Carolina. Some of Boyd's earliest published stories may date from before the war. See Chapter 2.

50. Manuscript version in Boyd Collection—Princeton. Quoted by permission.

51. Ms. in Boyd Collection—Princeton. Quoted by permission.

52. Letter of August [?], 1909; MSS—North Carolina.

53. From a typescript in Boyd Collection—Princeton.

54. Stanley Kunitz, *Living Authors* (New York, 1931), p. 52.

55. For an analysis of the most important stories, see Chapter 2.

56. See New York *Times Book Review,* April 5, 1925, p. 14; and New York *Times,* November 12, 1925, p. 4.

57. Boyd to Perkins, January 15, 1923; MSS—North Carolina.

58. Boyd to Perkins, December 28, 1924; Boyd correspondence in possession of Charles Scribner's Sons, Inc.

59. John Hall Wheelock, ed., *Editor to Author: The Letters of Maxwell Perkins* (New York, 1950), p. 42.

60. Review of *Drums,* New York *Evening Post,* April 11, 1925, p. 3. For a detailed analysis of *Drums,* see Chapter 3.

61. Figures based on correspondence in Scribner Papers and MSS—North Carolina. *Drums* sold more than nine thousand copies a year for fourteen years.

62. Cf. letters from Galsworthy to Boyd, June 4 and August 22, 1925; MSS—North Carolina.

63. James Southall Wilson, "The South Goes Democratic," *Saturday Review of Literature*, III (May 28, 1927), 860. For a detailed analysis of *Marching On*, see Chapter 3.

64. Cf. letter to Maxwell Perkins, November 2, 1929; Scribner Papers. For a detailed analysis of *Long Hunt*, see Chapter 4.

65. Letter to Ben Dixon MacNeill, February 23, 1932; MSS— North Carolina.

66. Jonathan Daniels, *Tar Heels* (New York, 1941), p. 219. For a detailed analysis of *Roll River*, see Chapter 5.

67. Parts of *Bitter Creek* had been published serially in the *Saturday Evening Post*, October 15-December 3, 1938. For an analysis of *Bitter Creek*, see Chapter 4.

68. The Free Company venture and its implications are discussed in detail in Chapter 7. For the plays themselves see James Boyd, ed., *The Free Company Presents* (New York, 1941). Like other writers, Boyd also lectured in behalf of the war effort, wrote for the Writers' War Board, and toward the end of the war, spoke at United Nations rallies. His 1941 address to the Canadian Club of Ottawa was published as "The South and the Fight," *Atlantic Monthly*, CLXXIII (February, 1944), 53-59.

69. For dates and places of publication of Boyd's poems, see Selected Bibliography.

70. Boyd to Green, July 19, 1943. Private papers of Paul Green. Quoted by permission. See Green's Preface to *Eighteen Poems*.

71. Published in *Atlantic Monthly*, CLXXIII (May, 1944), 67-68. Quotations used by permission.

72. Quotations from a letter to Laura Copenhaver, December 6, 1936; *Letters of Sherwood Anderson*, ed. by H. M. Jones and Walter B. Rideout (Boston, 1953), p. 368. Copyright 1953, by Eleanor Anderson. Quoted by permission of Little, Brown and Company. See Boyd's letter to Wolfe, December 8, 1936; Houghton Library of Harvard University. Copy in MSS—North Carolina.

73. Anderson to Perkins, February 3, 1937; *ibid.*, p. 371.

74. "Starting a Pack," *Country Life in America*, XXXIX (February, 1921), 57-58. Early in his career Boyd wrote frequently on hunting. See a series of articles in *Country Life in America*: "Beginner's Thoughts on Buying a Hunter," XXXVIII (September, 1920), 70-72; "Some Notes on Hunting Togs," XL (June, 1921), 48-49; and "Beginner's Thoughts on Crossing a Country," XL (September, 1921), 40-41. See also "Fox-hunting Accounted for . . .," *Vanity Fair*, XXX (March, 1928), 41ff.; "Free Rein to Folly . . .," *ibid.*, XXX (April, 1928), 75ff.; and "American Hunting and English Standards," *Cavalry Journal*, XXI (1931), 117-24.

75. "A Hunting We Will Go," *Magazine of the Southern Pines,* V (January, 1924), 3ff.

76. "Introduction" to *Hunting Sketches,* by Anthony Trollope (New York, 1933), pp. xviii-xix.

77. Letter of June 6, 1932; MSS—North Carolina.

78. Based on letter from Boyd to Schieffelin, May 29, 1831; MSS—North Carolina. I was not able to obtain a copy of the Dunbar *News* editorial.

79. "Strategy for Negroes," *The Nation,* CLVI (June 26, 1943), 884-87. All quotations are from this source.

80. Essentially the same argument is employed by C. Vann Woodward in "The North and the South of it," *The American Scholar,* XXXV (Autumn, 1966), pp. 657f. Boyd's argument was attacked in Horace R. Clayton's "The Negro's Challenge," *The Nation,* CLVII (July 3, 1943), 10-12.

81. "Novelist Editor," *Time Magazine,* XXXVII (May 26, 1941), 67.

82. A series of Boyd's liberal observations on the war and other current issues, written from the point of view of the rustic persona "Hugh Dave MacWhirr," was published in the *Pilot* during 1941-42, and subsequently as *Mr. Hugh Dave MacWhirr Looks After His $1.00 Investment in the Pilot Newspaper* (Southern Pines, N.C.; 1943).

83. This is not to suggest, of course, that either the eighteenth-century Virginia planter's democratic philosophy, or Boyd's, was without its inconsistencies—Thomas Jefferson's views on Negro slavery being a case in point, as is Boyd's treatment of Negroes in his stories (See Chapter 2). It is to say only that their view of the proper ordering of human society was basically democratic.

84. Letter to Charles Norman, May 20, 1916; MSS—North Carolina. Copy supplied by Charles Norman.

85. Southern Pines *Pilot,* June 25, 1943, p. 2.

86. Letter to American Civil Liberties Union, June 16, 1934; MSS—North Carolina.

87. Cf. Willard Thorpe, *American Writing in the Twentieth Century* (Cambridge, 1965), p. 133.

Chapter Two

1. "Learning the Craft," *The Editor,* LVI (January 28, 1922), 25-26.

2. See the posthumously published selection of the stories *Old Pines and Other Stories* (Chapel Hill, 1952).

3. The stories in this section are not necessarily discussed in chronological order. With two exceptions, all were published between

1921 and 1923, so that chronology is of little importance. As a rule, there is little evidence that they were published in the order of composition.

4. "The Sound of a Voice," *Scribner's Magazine*, LXX (August, 1921), 214-22. The story may have been begun as early as 1916, while Boyd was living in New York.

5. "The Verse on the Window," *Ladies Home Journal*, XXXIX (August, 1922), 10-11. Also in *Old Pines*, pp. 103-16. Quotations from latter source.

6. "The Superman," *Harper's Monthly Magazine*, CXLIV (March, 1922), 423-32.

7. "Out of the Mist," *Pictorial Review*, XXIII (January, 1922), 16ff. "Learning the Craft" was Boyd's statement of intention concerning this story.

8. "Uan the Fey," *Atlantic Monthly*, CXXIX (June, 1922), 790-96.

9. From an unpublished story of the series, "Eire from the Sea," in Boyd Collection—Princeton.

10. From manuscript notes in Boyd Collection—Princeton.

11. "Uan the Fey," *Atlantic Monthly*, CXXIX (June, 1922), 790.

12. "Bars," *Pictorial Review*, XXIII (August, 1922), 24, 26, 74. All quotations from this source.

13. "Luck," *Scribner's Magazine*, LXXIII (February, 1923), 173-78.

14. "The Flat Town" was probably written about 1922. A manuscript item in MSS—North Carolina indicates that it may have been published in 1934, but I have been unable to verify either place or date of publication. It appears in a perhaps slightly edited form in *Old Pines*, pp. 95-102, from which all quotations are taken.

15. "The Sound of a Voice," *Scribner's Magazine*, LXX (August, 1921), 220.

16. The example is in a sense unfortunate since the setting of "The Flat Town" apparently was not originally the coastal South. It was changed in order to make it fit in the *Old Pines* posthumous collection. The change is of little consequence, however, because the region described is very similar to Southern Pines.

17. "Old Pines," *Century Magazine*, CI (March, 1921), 609-18. Quotations are from *Old Pines*, pp. 3-27.

18. "Old Pines," in *Old Pines*, p. 3.

19. "Elms and Fair Oaks," *Scribner's Magazine*, LXX (November, 1921), 620-24.

20. "Shif'less," *Pictorial Review*, XXIV (February, 1923), 14ff. Quotations are from *Old Pines*, pp. 75-94.

21. "Bloodhound," *Scribner's Magazine*, XC (August, 1931), 209-11. Quotations are from *Old Pines*, pp. 46f.

22. "Civic Crisis," *American Mercury*, XLI (August, 1937), 468-80. Also in *Old Pines*, pp. 137-55, from which quotations are taken.

23. "Away! Away!," *Princeton University Library Chronicle*, VI (February, 1945), 62-76. Also in *Old Pines*, pp. 51-73, from which quotations are taken. Although published posthumously, the story was probably written in 1931 or 1932.

24. "The Gizzard of a Scientist," *Scribner's Magazine*, XCII (December, 1932), 327-32. Quotations are from *Old Pines*, pp. 117-36.

25. *Harper's Magazine*, CLXXXVIII (January, 1944), 450-57.

26. Boyd changed considerably in his attitude toward Negroes later in his career, as is clear from "Strategy for Negroes," *The Nation*, CLVI (June 26, 1943), 884-87; but little of the change is reflected in his belletristic writings. A notable exception is the poem "The Black Boys," in *Eighteen Poems* (New York, 1944), pp. 4-5. On "Strategy for Negroes," see Chapter 1.

Chapter Three

1. Letter to Edward B. Yeomans, Nov. 27, 1922; MSS—North Carolina.

2. The *Oxford Companion to American Literature* (3rd ed.; New York, 1956), for instance, in an entry on John Paul Jones, lumps *Drums* together with Winston Churchill's *Richard Carvel* and Cooper's *The Pilot* as "historical romances."

3. *Tar Heels* (New York, 1941), p. 219.

4. From an MS fragment, "The North Carolinian," in MSS— North Carolina.

5. Cf. Stanley Kunitz, *Living Authors* (New York, 1931), p. 52; New York *Times Book Review*, April 5, 1925, p. 14; and New York *Times*, November 12, 1925, p. 18; and four letters from Galsworthy to Boyd (1925-30), MSS—North Carolina.

6. Cf. Roger Burlingame, *Of Making Many Books* (New York, 1946), pp. 32, 63-64. Burlingame quotes portions of letters between Boyd and Perkins. One complete letter of December, 1924, is in John Hall Wheelock, ed., *Editor to Author* (New York, 1950), pp. 41f.

7. Review of *Drums* in the *Literary Review* of the New York *Evening Post*, April 11, 1925, p. 3.

8. Review in the *Literary Digest of the International Review of Books*, May 25, 1925, p. 400. Cf. letters to Boyd from John Galsworthy, June 4, 1925, and August 22, 1925; MSS—North Carolina.

9. Review in the *Bookman*, LXI (June, 1925), p. 470.

10. Review by Stallings in Harrisburg *Patriot*, March 31, 1925. From a clipping in MSS—North Carolina. *Richard Carvel* had gone through at least three editions and many reprintings by the time *Drums* appeared.

11. All quotations are from the "new uniform edition" of *Richard Carvel* (New York, 1927).

12. James Boyd, *Drums* (New York, 1925), p. 54. Subsequent references given in parentheses in text.

13. Such a reciprocal definition as a mark of excellence in the modern historical novel has been described in somewhat similar terms by Louis D. Rubin in "The Image of an Army: Southern Novelists and the Civil War," *Texas Quarterly*, I (Spring, 1958), 20ff.

14. Warren I. Titus, *Winston Churchill* (New York, 1963), pp. 32ff., indicates that Churchill's research for *Richard Carvel* was thorough and professional; but one feels solid historical ground beneath his feet only once, in the interpolated "Brief Summary, Which Brings This Biography to the Famous Fight Between the *Bonhomme Richard* and the *Serapis*" (pp. 443-46), which Churchill was either unwilling or unable to incorporate into the actual fabric of the novel.

15. See Struthers Burt, "James Boyd, '10," *Princeton University Library Chronicle*, VI (February, 1945), 59. Information on Boyd's research for *Drums*, as well as for his later novels, is based unless otherwise indicated, on a microfilm of his research card file lent me by the University of North Carolina Library. The film, "James Boyd Index Record," will hereafter be referred to as Boyd Index.

16. On the "pasteboard" characters of *Richard Carvel*, cf. Titus, *Winston Churchill*, pp. 41f.

17. For reviews that mentioned the historical aspects of *Drums* in particular, see the *Literary Review* of the New York *Evening Post*, April 11, 1925, p. 3; the Boston *Evening Transcript*, April 15, 1925, p. 4; the New York *Tribune*, May 31, 1925, p. 3; and the London *Times Literary Supplement*, October 22, 1925, p. 700.

18. For Perkins's response, see his letter of January 6, 1927, in *Editor to Author*, pp. 49f.

19. Review of *Drums* in the *Literary Review* of the New York *Evening Post*, May 14, 1927, p. 5.

20. James Southall Wilson, "The South Goes Democratic," *Saturday Review of Literature*, III (May 28, 1927), 860.

21. Fraser is a descendant of Johnny Fraser in *Drums*, but the fact is not of importance in the novel.

22. "The Rise and Fall of the Old Southern Illusion," *Brentano's Book Chat*, VI (September-October, 1927), 20f.

23. Such a statement is alluded to in Perkins's letter to Boyd of March 14, 1927; *Editor to Author*, p. 51. Quotation is from a letter from Boyd to DeVoto, January 27, 1938; MSS—North Carolina.

24. Preface to *Richard Carvel* (New York, 1927), ix.

25. Letter to DeVoto, January 27, 1938; MSS—North Carolina. Cf. DeVoto, "Fiction Fights the Civil War," *Saturday Review of Literature*, XVII (December 18, 1937), 16.

26. Cf. Wilson, *Saturday Review of Literature*, III (May 28, 1927), 860.

27. Letter to DeVoto, January 27, 1938; MSS—North Carolina.

28. Stephen Vincent Benét, *John Brown's Body* (New York, 1927), p. xii.

29. *Marching On* (New York, 1927), p. 6. Subsequent references indicated by page numbers in parentheses.

30. Metaphorically, the antagonism is suggested by the fact that the rough work he has to do makes his hands too large and insensitive to play the fiddle.

31. Some imagery associated with Stewart is nearly identical with that associated with Daisy. Cf. especially pp. 15 and 74.

32. "The Rise and Fall of the Old Southern Illusion," p. 21.

33. Robert A. Lively, *Fiction Fights the Civil War* (Chapel Hill, 1957), p. 184. In this respect *Marching On* is distinct from most Civil War novels, which, as Louis D. Rubin has said in "The Image of an Army," p. 24, portray the social system "for all its faults" as being "preferable to that which followed it."

34. Lively, p. 4.

35. *Ibid.*, pp. 47-64.

36. *Ibid.*, p. 21. Of the forty-five novels Lively considers the best, only *Marching On* and Evelyn Scott's *The Wave* were published in the 1920's. The latter, as Louis D. Rubin has suggested in "The Image of an Army," is conventional in handling the war on a panoramic scale.

37. Bernard DeVoto, "Fiction Fights the Civil War," *Saturday Review of Literature*, XVII (December 18, 1937), 4. The categories were originally DeVoto's, but they form the basis for much of Lively's analysis.

38. Lively, p. 81.

39. Thomas J. Pressly, *Americans Interpret Their Civil War* (Princeton, 1954), *passim.*

40. Charles A. Beard, *The Rise of American Civilization* (2 vols., New York, 1927). Cf. chapters XVII-XVIII. Remarks based on Pressly, pp. 187ff.

41. "Strategy for Negroes," *The Nation*, CLVI (June 26, 1943), 886.

42. Lively, p. 64 and *passim.* On the general implications of the Agrarian thesis for Civil War novels, see DeVoto, "Fiction Fights the Civil War," pp. 15f.

43. Lively, p. 38. Quoted from Stanley Kunitz, *Twentieth Century Authors* (New York, 1942), p. 172. On Boyd's house, which was not a copy of "Westover," see "Author of *Drums* Builds a House," *Arts and Decorations*, L (September, 1939), 12-14.

44. "The Rise and Fall of the Old Southern Illusion," *Brentano's Book Chat,* VI (September-October, 1927), 19.

45. Cf. Pressly, pp. 229ff.

46. I am aware that I am both accepting Lively's general analysis of Civil War novels and questioning some of its conclusions for *Marching On.* I consider this combination to be in no sense a contradiction since, in being obliged to read (he himself says "survey" would in some cases have been a better verb) 512 Civil War novels, Lively was denied the leisure I have had to read one very closely.

47. Lively, p. 186. Cf. DeVoto, "Fiction Fights the Civil War," pp. 15f.

48. *Ibid.,* p. 117.

49. *Ibid.,* p. 117.

50. Bernard DeVoto, "Escape to the West," *Saturday Review of Literature,* XIX (March 18, 1939), 6.

Chapter Four

1. *Marching On,* p. 257. Cf. p. 268.

2. Letter to Perkins, August 6, 1927; Scribner Papers.

3. See his letters to Perkins, December 15, 1928, and November 2, 1929. For Perkins's reactions to the novel, see John Hall Wheelock, ed., *Editor to Author: The Letters of Maxwell E. Perkins* (New York, 1950), pp. 65ff. Cf. Bernard DeVoto's comment that "it would not be absurd to call [*Long Hunt*] the best historical novel of our time," in *Saturday Review of Literature,* XIX (March 18, 1939), 6; and Thomas Wolfe's letter to Boyd, April 17, 1930 (MSS—North Carolina; published in Elizabeth Nowell, ed., *The Letters of Thomas Wolfe* [New York, 1956], pp. 225-26).

4. *Long Hunt* (New York, 1930), p. 4. Subsequent references by page number within the text.

5. Review in the *Saturday Review of Literature,* VI (June 14, 1930), 1127.

6. Review in the New York *Times Book Review,* April 6, 1930; p. 9.

7. Other reviewers disagreed. Ben Wasson (in *The Nation* [CXXXI, August 13, 1930]) found Rinnard an "independent and unsentimentalized . . . hero." Chamberlain's comment is closer to the truth, as the reviewer for the New York *Evening Post* agreed (April 11, 1930, p. 11).

8. Only one episode in the novel seems to have been based on actual historical events. The siege of the fort (pp. 357ff.) is in some respects similar to the siege of Boonesboro in 1778. (Cf. "The Siege of Boonesboro," in *The Siege of Boonesboro as Depicted by Stanley Arthurs and Interpreted by Fifty Authors* [Philadelphia, 1935], pp.

94-96.) In the novel, the siege occurs some thirty years later in a different part of the frontier. Boone himself never appears in the novel, nor does Rinnard bear any strong resemblance to him.

9. Salem was an eighteenth-century Moravian town. Winston was founded in 1849, but the two were not joined and called Winston-Salem until 1913.

10. Cf. Edwin Fussell, *Frontier: American Literature and the American West* (Princeton, 1965), p. 9.

11. Cf. Fussell, *Frontier*, p. 57. Cf. also Lucy Lockwood Hazard, *The Frontier in American Literature* (3rd ed., New York, 1961), pp. 111-12. Originally published 1927. In *Long Hunt*, cf. esp. p. 100.

12. James Fenimore Cooper, *The Prairie* (1827), ed. by H. N. Smith (New York, 1950), p. 8.

13. Cf. Hazard, pp. 109-12; and Fussell, p. 56.

14. Cf. Hazard, p. 111.

15. In conventional terms, Elizabeth Madox Roberts's *The Great Meadow* (1930) is more historical than *Long Hunt*. Many historical personages appear (Daniel Boone, Colonel Henderson, George Rogers Clark, and others), and a rather ineffectual attempt is made to relate the events of the plot to the major historical events of the period (cf. pp. 66, 96, and 125, for instance).

16. *The Great Meadow*, p. 110. Subsequent references in parentheses in text.

17. [August?], 1908; MSS—North Carolina.

18. See Chapter 5.

19. Cf. Julian R. Meade, "James Boyd," *Saturday Review of Literature*, XII (June 29, 1935), 11. Boyd had worked briefly with the West in his short story "Slim," published in *McCall's Magazine*, LIII (January, 1926), 9ff.

20. Portions of the novel appeared serially in the *Saturday Evening Post*, CCXI (October 15-December 3, 1938).

21. Bernard DeVoto, "Horizon Land (1)," *Saturday Review of Literature*, XIV (October 17, 1936), 8; and "Horizon Land (2)," *ibid.*, XV (April 24, 1937), 8. Rhodes's Western novels included *Good Men and True* (1910), *West is West* (1917), *Once in the Saddle* (1927), and *The Proud Sheriff* (1935). Richter published *The Sea of Grass* in 1937.

22. New York *Times Book Review*, March 19, 1939, p. 3.

23. Review in the Winnipeg *Free Press*, April 22, 1939. From a clipping in MSS—North Carolina.

24. Carl Van Doren, *The American Novel, 1789-1939* (New York, 1940), p. 362. Van Doren incorrectly gives the title as *Bitter River*.

25. Bernard DeVoto, "Escape to the West," *Saturday Review of Literature*, XIX (March 18, 1939), 6.

26. Review in the London *Times Literary Supplement,* March 23, 1940, p. 145.

27. *Bitter Creek* (New York, 1939), p. 18. Subsequent references given in parentheses in text.

28. Ray's responses to women can to a degree be analyzed in Freudian terms (cf. pp. 16, 70, 75, 380, for instance), but the intensity of Freudian motifs in the novel is not sufficient to warrant full analysis here.

29. Cf. Fussell, *Frontier.* Both earlier and later writers are treated in Robert Edson Lee, *From West to East: Studies in the Literature of the American West* (Urbana, Ill., 1966).

30. The early development of the Western is discussed in Moady C. Boatright, "The Beginnings of Cowboy Fiction," *Southwest Review,* LI (Winter, 1966), 11-28.

31. Owen Wister, *The Virginian* (rev. ed., New York, 1904), pp. ix and 84, respectively. Subsequent references given by page numbers in parentheses.

32. See James K. Folsom's cogent argument in *The American Western Novel* (New Haven, 1966), pp. 106ff.

33. *Ibid.,* pp. 13-16.

34. Based on Boyd Index. Titles and categories are representative only; the full bibliography for *Bitter Creek* includes nearly one hundred titles.

35. Folsom, p. 204.

36. See Henry Nash Smith, *The Virgin Land: The American West as Symbol and Myth* (Cambridge, 1950). Smith's mythic interpretation of the West in fiction is now so well established in criticism that it is frequently employed without documentation as an obvious fact. See for instance John Milton, "The Novel in the American West," *South Dakota Review,* II (Autumn, 1964), 56-76. Cf. Folsom, pp. 29-34.

37. Folsom, pp. 90-97, *passim.*

38. Folsom concludes from his examination of a large number of Western novels that there is "very little Western literature of even a faintly nihilistic moral tone." *Ibid.,* p. 122.

39. "Freedom and Destiny in the Myth of the American West," *New Mexico Quarterly,* XXXIII (Winter, 1963-64), 381-87.

Chapter Five

1. Letter to Horace Clute, July 10, 1935; MSS—North Carolina.

2. *Ibid.*

3. A telegram from Boyd to Perkins, March 14, 1934, asks the printer to change the name "Bond" to "Rand" and "Front Street" (the street the Boyds lived on in Harrisburg) to "River Street" throughout the manuscript.

4. Manuscript in Boyd Collection—Princeton. The outline dates perhaps from the early 1920's. Cf. the analyses of "Luck," "Uan Shane," and "The Flat Town," in Chapter 2. It is possible to see *Long Hunt, Drums,* and *Marching On* as related to the three "ages."

5. Cf. letter to Horace Clute, July 10, 1935; MSS—North Carolina. See also a letter from Thomas Wolfe to Boyd, April 23, 1934, in Elizabeth Nowell, ed., *The Letters of Thomas Wolfe* (New York, 1956), pp. 407f.

6. Letter to Paul Green, July 12, 1934; MSS—North Carolina.

7. Letter of February 23, 1932; MSS—North Carolina.

8. "The Dark Shore," *Scribner's Magazine,* XCV (May, 1934), 332ff.; XCV (June, 1934), 400ff.; XCVI (July, 1934), 16ff.; XCVI (August, 1934), 89ff. In *Roll River,* Book I contains three additional chapters. On the writing of Book II, see Maxwell Perkins's letter of June 25, 1934, in John Hall Wheelock, ed., *Editor to Author* (New York, 1950), p. 89.

9. Reviewed by Louise Field in the New York *Times Book Review,* April 28, 1935; p. 7. Some remarks suggest that the reviewer had not read the novel very carefully.

10. Bernard DeVoto, "A Novel Hammered Out of Experience," *Saturday Review of Literature,* XI (April 27, 1935), 645ff. All subsequent quotations from DeVoto are taken from this review. See Boyd's letter to Perkins, May 23, 1935; Scribner Papers.

11. See Wolfe's letter to Boyd of July 8, 1935, in Nowell, ed., *Letters,* p. 473; and to Kent Roberts Greenfield, June 23, 1936, *ibid.,* pp. 528ff.

12. Jonathan Daniels, *Tar Heels* (New York, 1941), p. 219. See Wolfe's letter to Daniels of October 23, 1936, in Nowell, ed., *Letters,* p. 551.

13. See letter from Boyd to Wolfe, January 9, 1930, Houghton Library of Harvard University. Wolfe requested recommendations from Perkins, Boyd, Robert A. Norwood, and Professor Homer A. Watt. See Elizabeth Nowell, *Thomas Wolfe: A Biography* (New York, 1960), p. 161. For Wolfe's reply to Boyd's letter, see Nowell, ed., *Letters,* p. 217.

14. See a long letter of July 1, 1930, from Wolfe to Perkins, in Nowell, ed., *Letters,* pp. 237-40.

15. See John Skally Terry, ed., *Thomas Wolfe's Letters to His Mother* (New York, 1943), p. 317; and Nowell, ed., *Letters,* p. 604.

16. See Boyd's letter to Perkins, November 25, 1929; Scribner Papers. Parts of Boyd's letter are quoted in Nowell, *Thomas Wolfe,* p. 156, and in Roger Burlingame, *Of Making Many Books* (New York, 1946), p. 16.

17. Wolfe to Boyd, January 12(?), 1930. Nowell, ed., *Letters,* p. 217.

18. Wolfe to Boyd, April 23, 1934; *ibid.*, p. 407. For an influence of a different kind, see Wolfe's letter on *Long Hunt* (1930), in *ibid.*, pp. 225ff.

19. See letters to Perkins, November 2, 1929, and December 14, 1935; Scribner Papers. See also Perkins's letter to Geoffrey Parsons, December 4, 1944, in *Editor to Author*, p. 257.

20. Cf. especially a letter to Perkins of August 4, 1934, Scribner Papers; and a letter of October 10, 1938, in Pack Memorial Public Library, Asheville, North Carolina.

21. Bernard DeVoto, "A Novel Hammered Out of Experience," *Saturday Review of Literature*, XI (April 27, 1935), 645.

22. *Roll River* (New York, 1935), pp. 3-4. Subsequent references given in parentheses within the text.

23. Cf. Ray M. Bertram, "James Boyd and the Impact of Change," *Boston University Studies in English*, III (Spring, 1957), 108-16.

24. On Clara as a source of accumulated wisdom in *Roll River*, see F. Scott Fitzgerald's letter to Boyd of May 2, 1935, in Andrew Turnbull, ed., *The Letters of F. Scott Fitzgerald* (New York, 1963), pp. 521ff.

25. Maxwell Perkins felt with some justice that Tommy's character was flawed by too great a passivity. See his letter to Boyd, June 25, 1934; *Editor to Author*, p. 89.

26. The homogeneity of the upper class is intentional and thematically functional. Cf. Bernard DeVoto, "Escape to the West," *Saturday Review of Literature*, XIX (March 18, 1939), 6.

27. *Saturday Review of Literature*, XI (April 27, 1935), 649.

28. Cf. Richard Gill, "The Imagination of Disaster," *Saturday Review*, XLVII (September 5, 1964), 10-13.

29. Bernard DeVoto, "A Novel Hammered Out of Experience," *Saturday Review of Literature*, XI (April 27, 1935), 645.

30. Cf. Robert L. Heilbroner, *The Future as History* (New York, 1960).

Chapter Six

1. Letter to Anderson, January 24, 1937; MSS—North Carolina.

2. Based on Green's personal diary, March 16, 1939. Used by permission.

3. See letter from Carl Carmer of the American Civil Liberties Union to Boyd, October 28, 1940; MSS—North Carolina.

4. Memorandum to the attorney general of the United States, September 25, 1940; MSS—North Carolina.

5. *Ibid.* Where the original idea came from is not clear. It could have come from Paul Green, but it apparently did not. Boyd had also been discussing various possibilities with his friend Francis

Biddle, who was solicitor general, and through whom he apparently first approached the attorney general. See Biddle's remarks on the episode in his autobiography, *In Brief Authority* (New York, 1962), pp. 124-26. See also letters from Boyd to Robert Sherwood, October 2, 1940; from Francis Biddle to Boyd, October 7, 1940; and from Boyd to David Lawrence, February 17, 1941; all in MSS—North Carolina.

6. Memorandum to attorney general, September 25, 1940; MSS—North Carolina.

7. See James Boyd, ed., *The Free Company Presents* (New York, 1941), p. vii; and his letter to Supreme Court Justice Felix Frankfurter, October 28, 1940; MSS—North Carolina. The entire official correspondence of the Free Company is in MSS—North Carolina.

8. Based on a series of letters between Boyd and Maxwell Perkins; MSS—North Carolina.

9. See letters between Boyd and Russel Crouse, January-February, 1941; MSS—North Carolina. Boyd still felt as late as mid-February that O'Neill would eventually join.

10. *The Free Company Presents*, p. vii.

11. Letter to Green, February 13, 1941; MSS—North Carolina.

12. An insignificant item, "Propaganda Is Assailed," appeared in the New York *Times*, February 2, 1941, p. 12. See Boyd's letters to Burgess Meredith, February 17 and April 23, 1941; MSS—North Carolina.

13. Cf. letters to Boyd from Francis Henry, January 26, 1941; and Arthur Krock of the New York *Times*, February 18, 1941; both in MSS—North Carolina.

14. Letter of February 18, 1941; MSS—North Carolina.

15. See *The Free Company Presents*, pp. 1-23. Subsequent references (given in parentheses within the text) are to this collection of the Free Company plays. Quotations used by permission of Dodd, Mead & Co.

16. Letter of February 26, 1941; MSS—North Carolina. Fifteen hundred letters came in to the Free Company office within a few days, most of them praising the broadcasts.

17. See letter to Boyd, March 2, 1941; MSS—North Carolina.

18. Another play Boyd wrote for the series, *Jim Crow*, was not produced.

19. On the story, see Parry Stroud, *Stephen Vincent Benét* (New York, 1962), pp. 120-22. On Benét's later work in behalf of the war effort, see *ibid.*, pp. 151ff.

20. The March 30 broadcast, a dramatization of Walter Van Tilburg Clark's *The Ox-Bow Incident* (1940), remains an enigma. Almost no record of it survives in the Free Company correspondence,

and it was not published in *The Free Company Presents*. See letter from Dodd, Mead & Co. to Boyd, April 10, 1941; MSS—North Carolina.

21. For a summary of Hearst's campaign against Welles, see *The New Republic*, CIV (February 24, 1941), 270f. Welles of course denied that Kane resembled Hearst, but Hearst had the poor judgment to insist that the film libeled him.

22. See *The New Republic*, CIV (March 10, 1941), 327.

23. See Meredith's telegram to Boyd, April 21, 1941; MSS—North Carolina.

24. *Time*, XXXVII (April 28, 1941), 80. Failure to locate accessible files of Hearst newspapers has made it necessary to rely heavily on this account of the Hearst campaign. All information used here, and not specifically attributed to another source, is from *Time*. So far as I was able to determine from other sources, the account is essentially correct. In keeping with the magazine's usual editorial policy, however, it may be slightly overstated.

25. Letter from Warner to Boyd, April 22, 1941; MSS—North Carolina.

26. Boyd to Warner, April 23, 1941; MSS—North Carolina.

27. New York *Times*, May 3, 1941; p. 6.

28. Later published in *Salvation on a String* (1946).

29. *The Free Company Presents*, p. vii.

30. Title was supplied by Boyd, who completed the play from a rough draft Anderson sent him late in January. Anderson died in the Canal Zone on March 8, before he finished the script for the broadcast. Boyd and Anderson were friends for about five years before the Free Company was formed. See Anderson's letters to Boyd in Howard M. Jones and Walter B. Rideout, eds., *Letters of Sherwood Anderson* (Boston, 1953). Boyd's tribute to Anderson was published as "A Man in Town," *Story*, XIX (September-October, 1941), 88ff.

31. Carl J. Friedrich, "The Poison in Our System," *Atlantic Monthly*, CLXVII (June, 1941), 668.

32. Boyd's letter of May 22, 1941, to Paul Green says that Columbia would have been willing to continue the series "indefinitely" if scripts had been available.

33. See Boyd's letter to MacLeish, May 27, 1941; MSS—North Carolina.

34. Francis J. Biddle, *In Brief Authority*, pp.124ff. Biddle gives no date or source for the announcement, and I have been able to discover none. Letters in MSS—North Carolina carry no such suggestion.

35. Radio station WNYC in New York gave live performances of ten of the eleven plays early in 1942. (Walter Clark's *The Ox-Bow*

Incident was excluded.) Commenting on the revival, John Hutchins called the plays "a gallant and prophetic chapter in radio history" (New York *Times*, February 15, 1942, p. 12).

36. Archibald MacLeish, "The Irresponsibles," in *The Nation*, CL (May 18, 1940), 618-23. All quotations from this source.

37. Van Wyck Brooks and John Gould Fletcher, letters to *The Nation*, CL (June 8, 1940), 718; and CL (June 22, 1940), 766, respectively. Brooks expanded his letter into an address at Hunter College in October, published as *On Literature Today* (New York, 1941). The public has a right, he said, extending MacLeish's argument, "to expect from its poets and thinkers some light on the causes of our problems and the way to a better future. Few writers . . .at present, are living up to these expectations" (9). If writers who are obsessed by a "death-drive" destroy "our will to make the world worth living in, we cannot let their influence go unchallenged" (18), Brooks argued.

38. See a series of letters in *The Nation*, CL (June 1, 1940), 678ff. Max Lerner said that "The writer's power to defend and change cultures is never great unless it is . . . linked with the expansive . . . forces in a culture" (678), and Waldo Frank maintained that the problem, far from being modern, has existed since the sixteenth century. Neither Lerner nor Frank questioned the propriety of the writer's accepting the responsibility MacLeish placed upon him; they merely questioned his ability to exercise it effectively.

39. James T. Farrell, "Literature and Ideology," in *The League of the Frightened Philistines* (New York, 1945), pp. 90-105. The essay was written in 1942. Cf. Ernest Hemingway's Introduction to *Men at War* (1942). See also Dwight MacDonald's reply to MacLeish in *Partisan Review*, VIII (November-December, 1941), 442-51; Edmund Wilson, "Archibald MacLeish and 'the Word,'" *New Republic*, CIII (July 1, 1940), 30ff.; Burton Rascoe, "The Tough-Muscled Boys of Literature," *American Mercury*, LI (November, 1940), 369; and Morton Zabel, "The Poet on Capitol Hill," *Partisan Review*, VIII (January, 1941), 1-17.

40. Allen Tate, "To Whom Is the Poet Responsible," in *The Man of Letters in the Modern World* (New York, 1955), pp. 23-33. Tate questioned the assumptions and conclusions of the MacLeish argument but said he could not "wholly dismiss" it.

41. Harold Clurman, *The Fervent Years* (London, 1946), p. 18.

42. *Ibid.*, p. 72.

43. Cf. Morgan Y. Himelstein, *Drama Was a Weapon* (New Brunswick, N.J., 1963), and especially the Foreword by John Gassner.

44. See, for instance, letters to Boyd of April 21 and May 20, 1941; MSS—North Carolina.

Chapter Seven

1. Hervey Allen, "History and the Novel," *Atlantic Monthly,* CLXXIII (February 9, 1944), 119. Quoted by Robert A. Lively, *Fiction Fights the Civil War,* p. 8.

2. Bernard DeVoto, "Escape to the West," *Saturday Review of Literature,* XIX (March 18, 1939), 6.

Selected Bibliography

PRIMARY SOURCES

The only previous bibliography of Boyd's writings appeared in *The Princeton University Library Chronicle*, VI (February, 1945), 77-81. The list that follows includes a number of items not found there, but does not include all of Boyd's editorials and articles (most of them unsigned) in the Southern Pines *Pilot*, 1941-43.

1. Novels and Collections

Drums. New York and London: Charles Scribner's Sons, 1925; New York: Charles Scribner's Sons, 1928; New York: Grosset and Dunlap, 1929; New York: Charles Scribner's Sons, 1936.
Marching On. New York: Charles Scribner's Sons, 1927; London: Heinemann, 1928; New York: Grosset and Dunlap, 1931.
Long Hunt. New York: Charles Scribner's Sons, 1930; London: Jarrold, 1931; New York: Grosset and Dunlap, 1935.
Roll River. New York: Charles Scribner's Sons, 1935; London: Jarrold, 1936; New York: Grosset and Dunlap, 1937.
Bitter Creek. New York: Charles Scribner's Sons, 1939; London: Heinemann, 1940; New York: Grosset and Dunlap, 1941.
The Free Company Presents: A Collection of Plays About the Meaning of America. Edited with an introduction by James Boyd. New York: Dodd, Mead & Co., 1941. (Contains Boyd's play, *One More Free Man.*)
Mr. Hugh Dave MacWhirr Looks After His $1.00 Investment in the Pilot Newspaper. Southern Pines, N.C.: The *Pilot*, 1943. (Collection of sketches published in the *Pilot*, 1941-42.)
Eighteen Poems. Foreword by Paul Green. New York: Charles Scribner's Sons, 1944. (Posthumous collection.)
Old Pines and Other Stories. Chapel Hill: University of North Carolina Press, 1952.

2. Articles, Short Stories, and Poems

"University Life Here and Abroad," Harrisburg (Pa.) *Telegraph*, Nov. 8, 1912, p. 7.
"Beginner's Thoughts on Buying a Hunter," *Country Life in America*, XXXVIII (September, 1920), 70-72.

"Bird Shooting With a Camera," *Country Life in America,* XXXVIII (September, 1920), 34-41.

"Starting a Pack," *Country Life in America,* XXXIX (February, 1921), 57-58.

"Old Pines," *Century Magazine,* CI (March, 1921), 609-18. Also in Richard Walser, ed., *North Carolina in the Short Story.* Chapel Hill: University of North Carolina Press, 1948; Richard Walser, ed., *Short Stories from the Old North State.* Chapel Hill: University of North Carolina Press, 1959.

"Some Notes on Hunting Togs," *Country Life in America,* XL (June, 1921), 48-49.

"The Sound of a Voice," *Scribner's Magazine,* LXX (August, 1921), 214-22. (story)

"Beginner's Thoughts on Crossing a Country," *Country Life in America,* XL (September, 1921), 40-41.

"Elms and Fair Oaks," *Scribner's Magazine,* LXX (November, 1921), 620-24. Also in *New Confederate Short Stories.* Columbia, S.C.: University of South Carolina Press, 1954.

"Out of the Mist," *Pictorial Review,* XXIII (January, 1922), 16ff. (story)

"Learning the Craft," *The Editor,* LVI (January 28, 1922), 25-26.

"The Superman," *Harper's Monthly Magazine,* CXLIV (March, 1922), 423-32. (story)

"Uan the Fey," *Atlantic Monthly,* CXXIX (June, 1922), 790-96. (story)

"Bars," *Pictorial Review,* XXIII (August, 1922), 24ff. (story)

"The Verse on the Window," *Ladies' Home Journal,* XXXIX (August, 1922), 10-11. (story)

"Luck," *Scribner's Magazine,* LXXIII (February, 1923), 173-78. (story)

"Shif'less," *Pictorial Review,* XXIV (February, 1923), 14ff. Also in Walter B. Pitkin, *As We Are.* New York: Harcourt, Brace, 1923. (story)

"The House of Blocks," *Century Magazine,* CVI (September, 1923), 734-40. (story)

"A Hunting We Will Go," *Magazine of the Southern Pines,* V (January, 1924), 3ff.

"Slim," *McCall's Magazine,* LIII (January, 1926), 9ff. (story)

"The Rise and Fall of the Old Southern Illusion," *Brentano's Book Chat,* VI (September-October, 1927), 19-22. Also: *Princeton Alumni Weekly,* XXVIII (October 14, 1927), 71.

"Tastes in Fiction," *Outlook,* CXLVII (October 26, 1927), 249ff.

"Fox-hunting Accounted For," *Vanity Fair,* XXX (March, 1928), 41ff.

"Free Rein to Folly; the Opportunities in Various Sports—Notably Fox-hunting," *Vanity Fair,* XXX (April, 1928), 75ff.

"Humoresque," *Scribner's Magazine*, LXXXIII (April, 1928), 449-57. (story)

"Story of the Richard-Serapis Fight," *World Review*, VIII (February 4, 1929), 8ff.

"Prospect for American Literature," *Outlook*, CLII (August 7, 1929), 587ff.

[Article on Craft of writing] Josephine K. Piercy, ed., *Modern Writers at Work*. New York: Macmillan, 1930.

"American Hunting and English Standards," *Cavalry Journal*, XXI (1931), 117-24.

"Bloodhound," *Scribner's Magazine*, XC (August, 1931), 209-11. Also: N. B. Fagin, ed., *America Through the Short Story*. Boston: Little, Brown & Co., 1937; J. T. Frederick, comp., *Present-day Stories*. New York: Charles Scribner's Sons, 1941.

"Gizzard of a Scientist," *Scribner's Magazine*, XCII (December, 1932), 327-32. Also in A. P. Hudson *et al.*, eds., *Nelson's College Caravan*. New York: Nelson & Sons, 1936. (story)

"Introduction" to *Hunting Sketches*. Anthony Trollope. New York: Gosden Head, 1933. Limited edition.

"Introduction" to *Old Bethesda*. Bion H. Butler. New York: Grosset & Dunlap, 1933.

"A Friend in Hollywood," Raleigh (N.C.) *News and Observer*, February 12, 1933, p. 5.

"The Siege of Boonesboro," *The Siege of Boonesboro as Depicted by Stanley Arthurs and Interpreted by Fifty Authors*. Philadelphia: University of Pennsylvania Press, 1935.

"Civic Crisis," *American Mercury*, XLI (August, 1937), 468-80. (story)

"*Bonhomme Richard* Finds the Baltic Fleet." Russel Blankenship *et al.*, eds., *Contemporary Literature*. New York: Charles Scribner's Sons, 1938. (Chapter 43 of *Drums*)

"The Train Ride." Josephine K. Piercy, ed., *Modern Writers at Work*. New York: Macmillan, 1939. (Part of Chapter 17 of *Marching On*)

150th Anniversary 1790-1940 Newville, Pennsylvania, With a Fore-Word by James Boyd. No place; no publisher, 1940.

"A Man in Town," *Story*, XIX (September-October, 1941), 88-91. (Tribute to Sherwood Anderson)

["Men and the War"], Southern Pines *Pilot*, May 15, 1942, p. 1.

"Antietam." F. Van Wyck Mason, ed., *The Fighting American* ... *Stories of American Soldiers*. New York: Reynal & Hitchcock, 1943. (Chapters 32-33 of *Marching On*)

"Song for the Silent," *Atlantic Monthly*, CLXXI (May, 1943), 87. (poem)

"Democracy," Southern Pines *Pilot*, June 25, 1943, p. 2.

"Strategy for Negroes," *The Nation,* CLVI (June 26, 1943), 884-87.
"What America Means," Southern Pines *Pilot,* August 13, 1943, p. 1.
"Civilian Night Song," *Harper's Magazine,* CLXXXVII (November, 1943), 544. (poem)
"Wedding Anniversary," *Ladies Home Journal,* LX (November, 1943), 91. (poem)
"Erastus Cotton and His Life as a Slave," Southern Pines *Pilot,* November 19, 1943, p. 1.
"To a Butterfly," *Atlantic Monthly,* CLXXIII (January, 1944), 96-97. (poem)
"The South and the Fight," *Atlantic Monthly,* CLXXIII (February, 1944), 53-59.
"Horses in the Sky," *Harper's Magazine,* CLXXXVIII (April, 1944), 450-57. (story)
"Echoes of Earth," *Atlantic Monthly,* CLXXIII (May, 1944), 67-68. (poem)
"Story of a Race in Revolutionary Times." M. C. Self, ed., *A Treasury of Horse Stories.* New York: A. S. Barnes, 1945. (Chapter 21 of *Drums*)
"Answer, Sky," *Princeton University Library Chronicle,* VI (February, 1945), 61. (poem)
"Away! Away!," *Princeton University Library Chronicle,* VI (February, 1945), 62-76.

3. Manuscripts, Letters, and Reviews

"As the Soldier Sees It," *Saturday Review of Literature,* III (June 4, 1927), 880. Review of John W. Thomason, *Red Pants*; Elliot W. Springs, *Nocturne Militaire*; and Leonard Mason, *Three Lights from a Match.*
Letter concerning review of *Slag* by John McIntyre, New York *Times Book Review,* November 27, 1927, p. 26.
Review of William E. Brook, *Lee of Virginia. Princeton Alumni Weekly,* XXXV (April 8, 1932), 592.
Review of Ellen Glasgow, *Vein of Iron. Saturday Review of Literature,* XII (August 31, 1935), 5-6.
Review of Gordon Hall Gerould, *How to Read Fiction. Princeton Alumni Weekly,* XXXVII (May 28, 1937), 724.

The two most important collections of Boyd's papers and manuscripts are at Princeton University and in the Southern Historical Collection at the University of North Carolina. The former contains a few letters and all of the manuscripts of the novels. The latter contains most of the letters and personal papers, and manuscripts for many of the short stories.

SECONDARY SOURCES

This list includes only the most important books and articles. Consult Notes and References for complete list of all sources used, including reviews of individual works. Since very little has been written about Boyd, the most useful sources were his own published works, and the two major collections of correspondence and manuscripts.

BERTRAM, RAY M. "James Boyd and the Impact of Change," *Boston University Studies in English*, III (Spring, 1957), 108-16. General consideration of change as a motif in the novels.

BURLINGAME, ROGER. *Of Making Many Books*. New York: Charles Scribner's Sons, 1946. History of Scribner's. Numerous references to Boyd; quotations from his letters.

BURT, STRUTHERS. "James Boyd, '10," *Princeton Alumni Weekly*, XXXVI (November 22, 1935), 195-96. Reminiscence by Princeton professor who became Boyd's neighbor and friend in Southern Pines.

————. "James Boyd, 1888-1944," *Princeton University Library Chronicle*, VI (February, 1945), 56-60. Reminiscences.

DANIELS, JONATHAN. *Tar Heels*. New York: Dodd, Mead & Co., 1941. Contains some observations on literature in North Carolina in the 1920's, and on Boyd and Thomas Wolfe in particular.

DEVOTO, BERNARD. "Fiction and the Everlasting *If*: Notes on the Contemporary Historical Novel," *Harper's*, CLXXVII (June, 1938), 42-49. Excellent commentary on the historical novel as a form.

————. "Fiction Fights the Civil War," *Saturday Review of Literature*, XVII (December 18, 1937), 3ff. Defines categories used by Robert Lively for *Fiction Fights the Civil War* (1957).

FOLSOM, JAMES K. *The American Western Novel*. New Haven: College and University Press, 1966. Novels of the twentieth century.

FUSSELL, EDWIN S. *Frontier: American Literature and the American West*. Princeton: Princeton University Press, 1965. The West as a motif in nineteenth-century American literature.

JONES, HOWARD M. and WALTER B. RIDEOUT, eds. *Letters of Sherwood Anderson*. Boston: Little, Brown & Co., 1953. Five letters to Boyd.

LIVELY, ROBERT A. *Fiction Fights the Civil War*. Chapel Hill: University of North Carolina Press [1957]. Excellent treatment of Civil War novels, including *Marching On*.

MEADE, JULIAN R. "James Boyd," *Saturday Review of Literature*, XII (June 29, 1935), 10-11. Useful biographical information.

The Medical Department of the U. S. Army in the World War. 15

vols. Washington, D. C.: Surgeon General's Office, 1921-29. Vols. VII and VIII useful for the Ambulance Service.

NOWELL, ELIZABETH, ed. *The Letters of Thomas Wolfe.* New York: Charles Scribner's Sons, 1956. Four letters to Boyd.

The *Pilot.* Weekly newspaper of Southern Pines, North Carolina. Owned and edited by Boyd, 1941-44.

PRESSLY, THOMAS J. *Americans Interpret Their Civil War.* Princeton: Princeton University Press, 1954. Discusses historians' changing views on causes of the war.

WHEELOCK, JOHN HALL, ed. *Editor to Author, the Letters of Maxwell E. Perkins.* New York: Grosset & Dunlap, 1950. Letters of Boyd's editor. Four letters to Boyd.

Index

169

DATE DUE

3/13			
GAYLORD			PRINTED IN U.S.A